December 2001

Happy Holidays

To Our Friends & Clients

from all of us at

Manfredi, Levine & Eccles, APC

3262 E. Thousand Oaks Boulevard, Suite 200
Westlake Village, CA 91362
(805) 379-1919

The **100** Greatest Movies Of All Time

Top20

1-100 Contents

Editor in Chief **Norman Pearlstine**
Editorial Director **Henry Muller**
Chairman, CEO **Don Logan**
Executive Vice Presidents **Donald M. Elliman Jr., Elizabeth Valk Long, Jim Nelson, Joseph A. Ripp**

Managing Editor **James W. Seymore Jr.**
Executive Editors **Peter Bonventre, Richard Sanders**
Assistant Managing Editors **Mark Harris, Maggie Murphy, Mary Kaye Schilling**
Design Director **John Korpics** Photography Director **Mary Dunn**

L.A. Bureau Chief **Cable Neuhaus** Senior Editors **George Blooston, Doug Brod, Ty Burr, Jess Cagle, Tina Jordan, Albert Kim, John McAlley** Director of Research Services **Annabel Bentley** Editorial Manager **Louis Vogel** Staff Editors **Jamie Bufalino, Cynthia Grisolia** Critic-at-Large **Ken Tucker** Critics **David Browne, Bruce Fretts, Owen Gleiberman, Lisa Schwarzbaum** Writer-at-Large **Benjamin Svetkey** Senior Writers **Rebecca Ascher-Walsh, Betty Cortina, Steve Daly, Joe Flint, Jeff Gordinier, David Hochman, A.J. Jacobs, Noah Robischon, Chris Willman** Associate Editors **Marc Bernardin, Eileen Clarke, Dulcy Israel, Wook Kim, Alice King, Joe Neumaier, Jessica Shaw (L.A.), William Stevenson, Mitchell Vinicor, Tracy A. Walsh, Fan Wong** Staff Writers **Andrew Essex, Mike Flaherty, Jeff Jensen, Christopher Nashawaty, Tom Sinclair, Dan Snierson** Correspondents **Kristen Baldwin, Rob Brunner, Dave Karger, Deanna Kizis** Senior Broadcast Correspondent **Lisa Karlin**

DESIGN Art Director **Geraldine Hessier** Managing Art Directors **Joe Kimberling, John Walker** Assistant Art Directors **George McCalman, Jennifer Procopio, Liliane Vilmenay, Ellene Wundrok** Designers **Edith L. Gutierrez, Erin Whelan** Imaging Technician **Susan Van Over** Design Assistant **Lilah Nowick**

PICTURES Picture Editor **Doris Brautigan** Picture Editor, Special Projects **Sarah Rozen** Associate Picture Editor **Alice H. Babcock** West Coast Picture Editor **Michael Kochman** Assistant Picture Editors **Helena V. Ashton, Richard B. Maltz, Suzanne Regan, Michele Romero** Picture Coordinator **Luciana Chang** Assistant **L. Michelle Dougherty**

RESEARCH SERVICES Deputy **Tim Purtell** Senior Reporter **Beth Johnson** Reporters **Carmela Ciuraru, Leslie Marable, Joshua Rich, Erin Richter, Nancy Sidewater, Daneet Steffens, Lori L. Tharps** Information Center Manager **Rachel Sapienza** Deputy **Stacie Fenster** Senior Associate **Sean O'Heir** Assistant **Alexandria Carrion**

COPY Copy Chief **Ben Spier** Copy Editor **David Penick** EDITORIAL ASSISTANTS **Clarissa Cruz, Daniel Fierman, Gillian Flynn, Tricia Johnson, Will Lee, Shawna Malcom, Leonard McCants, Laura Morgan, Troy Patterson** ADMINISTRATION Assistant to the Managing Editor **Rita Silverstein** Staff **Carole Willcocks**

EW ONLINE Editor **Michael Small** Executive Editor **Mark Bautz** Producer **Barclay A. Dunn** Correspondents **Liane Bonin, Josh Wolk** Associate Producer **Stella Anastasia** Editorial Coordinator **Gary Eng Walk** Production Assistant **Connie Yu** Editorial Assistant **Sandra P. Angulo**

PRODUCTION Ad Production Manager **Sandra Rosano** Makeup Manager **Robin Kaplan** Operations Manager **Karen S. Doyle** Production Manager **Sue Barnett** Assistant Makeup Manager **Don Gordon** Assistant Operations Manager **Nicol D. DeVito** Imaging Operations Supervisor **Paul Bodley Jr.** Senior Production Associates **Ray Battaglino, George L. Beke, Evan J. Dong, John Goodman, Michael R. Hargreaves, John K. Horsky, Robert D. Kennedy, Bill Lazzarotti, Eileen M. O'Sullivan, Tom Roemlein, David Serrano, George Sumerak, Daniel C. Thompson** Production Coordinators **Ann Griffith O'Connor, Karen E. Sharp, Manga L. Tatini** Production Assistant **Christine W. Cheng**

TECHNOLOGY Manager **Jeffrey Cherins** Systems Administrator **Jason Schlau** Desktop Support Analysts **Godwin Mensah, Joe Russell**

CONTRIBUTORS **Judith I. Brennan, Pat H. Broeske, Caren Weiner Campbell, Heidi Siegmund Cuda, Vanessa V. Friedman, L.S. Klepp, Gene Lyons, Lois Alter Mark, Margot Mifflin, Jim Mullen, Alanna Nash, Lawrence O'Toole, Degen Pener, Ira Robbins, Michael Sauter, Stephen Schaefer, Bob Strauss**

President **John Squires**
Publisher **Michael J. Kelly**

Consumer Marketing Director **Monica Ray** Director of Finance & Administration **George H. Vollmuth** Director of Production & Technology **Carol A. Mazzarella** Associate Publisher **David S. Morris** Vice President, Marketing & Promotion **Fred O. Nelson** Director of Public Relations & Communications **Sandy W. Drayton**

CONSUMER MARKETING **William J. Stutzman** (Assistant Director); **Timothy M. Smith, Holley Vantrease, Vincent M. Vero** (Managers); **Matthew T. Chang, B.J. Casey; Eleanor Hong; Taleen Gergerian**

ADVERTISING SALES Headquarters **Thomas A. Morrissy** (Eastern Manager); **Grace Whitney** (Sales Development Director); **Carole S. Harnoff** (Classified Sales Manager); **Ellen Jacobson, Felice Pilchik** Atlanta **Andrew M. Davis** (Manager); **Melanie Oliva** Chicago **Philip A. Wertz** (Midwest Manager); **Brianne Bremer, Christopher S. White** (Sales Representatives); **Kelly D. Netzband** Detroit **Danielle Morris** (Manager); **Stephen C. Larson** (Sales Representative); **Maryanne Murawski** Los Angeles **Linda A. Villani** (Manager); **Kimberly Allen** (Associate Manager); **Kari Eisaman, Matthew J. Sganga** (Sales Representatives); **Deborah I. Gelfand, Sharon M. Gold** New York **Daryl P. Bowman** (National Fashion Director); **Raymond T. Chelstowski, Jodi H. Cohen, Melissa J. Nadler, Julie R. Schoenberg, Suzanne Speichinger** (Sales Representatives); **Catherine Cusack** San Francisco **Jacque Lapsey** (Manager); **Christine Connolly** (Sales Representative); **Michelle Murphy** Dallas **Jo Neese, Tammy Stilling** (Kelly/Tremblay & Company)

MARKETING & PROMOTION **Rose Bleszcz, Gail L. Chen, Karen Gottschalk, Kathleen A. Moore, Elizabeth A. Ronan** (Directors); **Steven T. Porter; Kelly Kim, Gloria H. Sutton** (Managers); **Dylan Parks, Mel Sanchez, Garnell Shumate, Jacqueline L. Stiles** Public Relations **Jason T. Averett, Hope E. Wilson**

FINANCE & ADMINISTRATION Finance **Stephanie B. Torre** (Director); **Sherry W. Burns; Beverly Ivens, Jane L. Koty, Richard J. Schexnider, Suzanne Shakter; Vivian Adamakos, Miriam T. Fernando** Administration **Ilissa R. Sternlicht** (Manager); **Sheila M. Kelly Sheila Drouet** Legal **Amy Glickman**

TIME INC.

Executive Editors **Joëlle Attinger, José M. Ferrer III** Development Editor **Jacob Young** Editor-at-Large **Daniel Okrent**

TIME INC. EDITORIAL SERVICES **Sheldon Czapnik** (Director); **Claude Boral** (General Manager); **Thomas E. Hubbard** (Photo Lab); **Lany Walden McDonald** (Research Center); **Beth Bencini Iskander, Kathi Doak** (Picture Collection); **Thomas Smith** (Technology)

TIME INC. EDITORIAL TECHNOLOGY **Paul Zazzera** (Vice President); **Damien Creavin** (Director)

About the Author

What was Alfred Hitchcock's best film? Can *Airplane!* be considered a classic? Do you dare mention *Chinatown* and *Pulp Fiction* in the same breath? ∎ These are the sort of questions ENTERTAINMENT WEEKLY staffers thrive on debating. At a publication crawling with obsessive movie buffs, opinions about what constitutes great cinema aren't hard to come by. So when we began planning this book—*The 100 Greatest Movies of All Time*— everyone had something to say. Eventually, a working list (whittled down from some

Editor **Peter Bonventre**
Design Director **John Korpics**
Photo Editor **Sarah Rozen**
Senior Writer **Ty Burr**

Senior Editors **Matthew McCann Fenton, Tim Purtell** Associate Editor **Bianca Perlman** Writers **Carmela Ciuraru, Eileen Clarke, Wook Kim, Allyssa Lee, Leslie Marable, Joe Neumaier, Joshua Rich, Erin Richter** Reporters **Jennifer Boeth, Amy Feitelberg, Karen Mancuso, Nancy Sidewater, Daneet Steffens** Photo Associate **Deborah Dragon** Copy Editors **Angie Argabrite, Mila Drumke, Cynthia McClean, David Penick**

Editorial Production Manager **David Serrano** Edit Production **Ray Battaglino, Paul Bodley Jr., Evan J. Dong, John Goodman, Michael R. Hargreaves, John K. Horsky, Robert D. Kennedy, Bill Lazzarotti, Eileen M. O'Sullivan, Tom Roemlein, George Sumerak, Daniel C. Thompson** Consumer Marketing Director **Monica Ray**

TIME INC. HOME ENTERTAINMENT
President **David Gitow**

Director, Continuities and Single Sales **David Arfine** Director, Continuities and Retention **Michael Barrett** Director, New Products **Alicia Longobardo** Director, Licensing **Risa Turken** Group Product Manager **Jennifer McLyman** Product Managers **Roberta Harris, Carlos Jimenez, Kenneth Maehlum, Daniel Melore** Manager, Retail and New Markets **Thomas Mifsud** Associate Product Managers **Daria Raehse, Dennis Sheehan, Meredith Shelley, Betty Su, Niki Viswanathan, Lauren Zaslansky, Cheryl Zukowski** Assistant Product Managers **Victoria Alfonso, Jennifer Dowell** Editorial Operations Director **John Calvano** Book Production Manager **Jessica McGrath** Assistant Book Production Manager **Jonathan Polsky** Book Production Coordinator **Kristen Travers** Fulfillment Director **Michelle Gudema** Associate Fulfillment Manager **Richard Perez** Financial Director **Tricia Griffin** Financial Manager **Amy Maselli** Assistant Financial Manager **Steven Sandonato** Marketing Assistant **Ann Gillespie**

Library Of Congress Catalog Number: 99-71058

We welcome your comments and suggestions about Entertainment Weekly Books. Please write to us at: Entertainment Weekly Books, Attention: Book Editors, P.O. Box 11016, Des Moines, IA 50336-1016

If you would like to order any of our hardcover collector-edition books, please call us at 1-800-327-6388. (Monday through Friday, 7 a.m.–8 p.m. or Saturday, 7 a.m.–6 p.m. Central time.)

500 choices) was decided upon, and executive editor Peter Bonventre began looking for a writer to put the whole shebang in context. ▪ He didn't have far to look. Senior editor Ty Burr—whose voluminous knowledge of filmic lore is legendary in these halls—seemed the obvious choice to critically assess these 100 disparate movies. "I needed someone to hit it out of the park," says Bonventre, "a go-to writer who had the wit, passion, knowledge—and energy—to get the job done. Putting the bat in Ty's hands was an easy call." ▪ Ty, who's been a film junkie since the day he caught *Duck Soup* on late-night TV as a kid in Massachusetts, eagerly agreed to take on the task. "It's kind of a natural for me," he says. "I've studied—and loved—these films for virtually my entire life." Indeed. As an undergraduate at Dartmouth, Ty ran the student film society and spent a transfer year studying cinema at NYU. After eight years programming movies ("mostly lousy ones," he says modestly) for Cinemax, he joined EW as a staff writer in 1991, where he has served as the magazine's chief video critic, film score expert, and resident Buster Keaton freak. ▪ As the mastermind behind EW's Multimedia section, he also keeps a close watch on the Internet, which he views as a vitally important new medium. Yet his love of the big screen remains his primary raison d'être. And now you'll get a chance to consider his takes on these classic films. Frankly, we're awed by the gusto with which he plunged into this daunting task—and delighted with the results. We think you will be, too.   PHOTOGRAPH BY ETHAN HILL

Introduction

Lists are silly.

There, we said it. You know it, we know it, and you're
still flipping through this book, aren't you? Because
making lists—and arguing over them—is some kind
of fundamental, genetically encoded human itch.
Anyway, when it comes to movies, how else to make
sense of all those visions pouring down on us? So
many films have been made in the past 100 years,
and so many have affected us, individually and as a
culture, that the temptation to rank is felt by buffs
and casual filmgoers alike. Even the august
American Film Institute deigned to weigh in, with a
recent "100 Years…100 Movies" roundup that
generated flares of controversy. (Come on, no
Preston Sturges?) But what list doesn't? How do you
jam all the worthies into a mere 100 slots? Who says
Gone With the Wind is a "better" movie than *Aliens*?
Who in their right mind would *compare* them?

Well… we would. Because if making a Greatest
Movies list is a patently absurd exercise, it's also
inherently useful. This is the parlor game that prompts
memory and appreciation, nudges us toward a shared
set of creative benchmarks, and, perhaps most
important, can be passed on to the moviegoing
neophyte with the words "Start here." It's that
concept—the 100 Greatest Films as a kind of "Movies
101"—that drives the book you're holding.

Who says *Gone With the Wind* is a "better" movie than *Aliens*? Who in their right mind would compare them?

When the ENTERTAINMENT WEEKLY staffers involved with this project corralled all the responses from our officewide e-mailing and set about the monumentally ridiculous task of boiling 500 nominated films down to an even 100, we saw our mission as both recognizing pure quality and, to a certain extent, offering a balanced snapshot of film history. Sure, you could come up with a top 10 made up entirely of Hitchcock movies—and it would arguably hold water—but think of all the films you'd have to displace. We also took it upon ourselves to correct some of the AFI list's more glaring omissions—you'll find Sturges, Buster Keaton, and two Ernst Lubitsch movies here—as well as to make room for the best filmmaking from other countries, on the understanding that a list that doesn't include Fellini, Truffaut, and Kurosawa has serious credibility problems.

What won't you find here? Short films, documentaries—or any movies from the last five years. The first two categories we left out because we had to draw the line somewhere if we didn't want to omit genuine classics of the feature-narrative form; we withheld judgment on more recent movies simply because greatness tends to emerge with time. (And yes, maybe we're wrong about *Pulp Fiction* and *The Piano*—could you let us know in a decade or so?)

It's important to realize, too, that while this book is about movies, it only tangentially celebrates the people *in* them. Once we'd assembled a top 100 that felt fair and right, we stood back and noted, with some shock, which actors were in and which were out. With five movies on our list, Jimmy Stewart is the most-represented male star—but two-time Oscar winner Spencer Tracy is nowhere to be seen. Cary Grant and Robert De Niro have four movies each—and so does Alec Guinness. You won't find Julia Roberts, Elizabeth Taylor, or Greta Garbo— but you will find Janet Leigh, who, with three films here, is this book's unofficial leading lady.

Which proves only that a great star vehicle is not necessarily the same thing as a great movie. Thankfully—and logically—our directors' inner circle looks a bit more sane: Hitchcock reigns with four movies in our top 100, followed by three each from Steven Spielberg, Martin Scorsese, David Lean, Michael Curtiz, and Billy Wilder.

Not that you should stop there. With any luck, EW's *The 100 Greatest Movies of All Time* will prompt you to build your own personal top 100, 200, 500... There are a lot of movies out there, and the dirty little secret is that even the bad ones can be great fun. In the end, this is just our way of indulging the primal list lust that, for all we know, goes back to the dawn of man. Somewhere, painted on the walls of an as-yet-undiscovered cave, there's a ranked tally of "The 100 Greatest Mammoth-Hunting Reenactments." And you can bet that it started arguments.

1

The Godfather *(1972)* Audiences had never seen such casual savagery—but this isn't our top pick because it was so shocking. Marlon Brando jump-started his career, while Al Pacino, James Caan, and Diane Keaton became superstars—but the cast is only part of its greatness. It so firmly laid down the rules of how the Mafia should be portrayed that nearly 30 years later, movies (*Analyze This*) and TV shows (*The Sopranos*) still work within its boundaries. But coining clichés isn't enough to make a film great. ■ Instead, *The Godfather* is here for its classicism, uncanny and—given the agonies involved in its making—unexpected. Director Francis Ford Coppola crafted a work that now seems to stand, Janus-faced, at the dividing line between old Hollywood and new, between the hushed control of the studio system and the noisy, grabby sprawl of today—between Michael Corleone silently marveling at the steadiness of his hand after facing down the men who had hoped to murder his father, and the unforgiving baptism of vengeance that closes the film. Above all, *The Godfather* is, along with its sequel and the film that follows it on this list, the truest and most unnerving picture of American striving—which is to say America itself—ever filmed. PHOTOGRAPHS BY STEVE SCHAPIRO

Oscar Index · Ten nominations; three wins (Best Picture, Best Actor, and Adapted Screenplay)

Cinema Vérité · The scene in which Sonny beats his brother-in-law senseless was genuinely violent: Caan broke two of Gianni Russo's ribs and chipped his elbow.

Gross-Out Vérité · The horse head was real. Prop scouts found a horse in a New Jersey rendering plant that was scheduled for slaughter and had its head shipped to the set in dry ice.

Character Notes · Brando based his characterization of Vito Corleone in part on wiretapped recordings of raspy-voiced Mafia kingpin Frank Costello.

Made Guys Have Feelings Too · At the urging of Mafia boss Joe Colombo, the producers agreed to remove the words *Mafia* and *La Cosa Nostra* from the script.

Citizen Kane

(1941) So entrenched
is Charlie Kane at the top of Greatest Movies
lists that neophytes may come away wondering
what all the fuss is about. (They probably
already know the identity of Rosebud through
cultural osmosis alone.) But that's a measure of
how thoroughly Orson Welles' once-scandalous
movie debut triumphed over the system that
destroyed its creator. *Kane* didn't revolutionize
the way movies were made—although deep-
focus camera work and overlapping dialogue
acquired powerful artistic cachet in Welles'
hands—so much as he changed *what* kinds
of stories were told, and *how*. Breezing into the
"toy train set" that was Hollywood, the boy
genius took as his first subject the life
of a media mogul—how's that for chutzpah?—
and found behind the tycoon's facade a hall of
mirrors that reflected the creative visionary,
the controlling lover, the blowhard politico, the
lost child, and the tired old man. *Kane* is
the first great work of pessimism to come out of
Hollywood—the first to locate the wounded,
bullying egotism behind the American dream—
but what's most remarkable nearly 60 years
later is the sheer, joyous verve of the thing. He
was only 25; how could Welles have known he
would live out his own version of the tale?

3

Casablanca *(1942)* Proof that the dream factory worked, even when nobody involved knew what the hell they were doing. The stories of how *Casablanca* came together almost in spite of itself—pages of dialogue arriving minutes before scenes were to be shot, actors filming reaction shots without knowing what they were reacting *to*— are fun but ultimately beside the point. The finished film is a complete thing: potent, instantly familiar, infinitely watchable. As Rick Blaine, master of the Café Américain, Bogart perfected his image as the burnt romantic we'd all like to be—watch how he holds himself in surly abeyance, then tumbles helplessly back into passion—but *Casablanca* is packed with additional riches: Sydney Greenstreet's phlegmatic Ferrari (Jabba the Hutt four decades ahead of schedule), Peter Lorre's scuttling Ugarte ("*Reeck!*"), Claude Rains' blithely corrupt Renault, Paul Henreid as that noble sap Victor Laszlo. And, breathing feeling back into the hero simply by showing up at his nightclub, Ingrid Bergman's incandescent Ilsa. ■ Do such characters exist in real life? Of course not; that's why Hollywood had to invent them. *Citizen Kane* may have showed up the average American film of its time as a nicely produced fib, but Bogart, Bergman, and director Michael Curtiz wrought the kind of lie that offers deeper comforts. Say what you will about today's trendy cinematic nihilism: We'll always have *Casablanca*.

Oscar Index · Eight nominations; three wins (Best Picture, Best Director, and Original Screenplay)

Original Casting · Producers initially considered Ronald Reagan as Rick, Ann Sheridan as Ilsa, and Lena Horne as Sam (whom they considered making a woman).

What Did They Know? · George Raft, who was passed over for Rick, is said to have groused, "I don't want to star opposite an unknown Swedish broad."

Another Idol With Clay Feet · Dooley Wilson (Sam) sang "As Time Goes By" beautifully, but he couldn't play "Chopsticks" on piano. Wilson mimes tickling the ivories during his scenes, and actual music was dubbed in later.

Oops! · Ilsa reminisces about the dress she wore the last time she saw Rick. But in the flashback, she wears a suit.

4

Chinatown *(1974)* Cold-blooded and tenderhearted, *Chinatown* stands out from all those smug, hippie neo-noirs of the mid-1970s like a shark in a fishpond. Everyone involved made crucial contributions. Jack Nicholson gave a performance of smart, reined-in power as L.A. private eye Jake Gittes—it's the polar opposite of the wacky Jack we love, and the better for it. As an entangled daughter-father duo, Faye Dunaway and John Huston are intensely moving and unfathomably evil, respectively. Writer Robert Towne's script is often, and rightly, held up as the modern model of the form: It weaves the nasty politics of how Los Angeles got its water during the 1930s into a fond genre reworking and somehow ends up a shattering human tragedy—all without losing its cool. Even Jerry Goldsmith's score is a brooding, sinuous landmark. ■ And yet, *Chinatown* is Roman Polanski's film. Period. The Polish expatriate (left, with Nicholson) may have been working in Hollywood, but he knew how capricious and cruel the real world could be. His mother had been killed by the Nazis during World War II; his wife had been butchered by the Manson family in 1969; there were other terrors in between. It was Polanski who insisted on rewriting the ending, who closes the trap on Evelyn Mulwray—and who leaves us on that crowded street with our childish hopes for happy endings mocked. ■ The film's penultimate line is "Forget it, Jake.... It's Chinatown." As if we could. PHOTOGRAPHS BY STEVE SCHAPIRO

5

Oscar Index · Eight nominations; two wins (Best Actor and Film Editing)

Making It Real · De Niro prepared for the role by sparring with LaMotta for a full year and giving the former champ multiple black eyes, several smashed teeth, and one cracked rib.

Second Chances · By the late 1970s, Joe Pesci had been through one career as an actor and had resigned himself to managing a restaurant. He was dragged out of retirement by De Niro and Scorsese.

Second Thoughts? · During fight training, De Niro also cracked two of Pesci's ribs.

First Impressions · LaMotta said of *Raging Bull*: "When I saw the film I was upset, I kind of look bad in it. Then I realized it was true. That's the way it was. I was a no-good bastard."

Raging Bull *(1980)* Is it at all surprising that *Raging Bull* lost the Best Picture Oscar to *Ordinary People*? Robert Redford's fine film is a dream of genteel, proto-yuppie healing, whereas Martin Scorsese's boxing bio is a howl from a storm drain. Redford probed the fissures in respectable folk; Scorsese went searching for nobility in a thoroughly despicable man. Which would *you* have given an award to? ■ Now, of course, it's easy to say. Nearly 20 years on, *Raging Bull* hasn't dated an iota, and not because Scorsese shot it in black and white. If anything, time has caught up with the film; once you've seen the story of Jake LaMotta's uncomprehending rise and self-immolating fall, doesn't Mike Tyson's career make sense? ■ From the standpoint of sheer craft, it's tough to say what's more impressive—Scorsese's direction or Robert De Niro's performance. *Raging Bull*'s boxing sequences stand with the greatest moments in movie history, and, crazy with vicious poetry, they're true to the sport. De Niro underwent a celebrated physical transformation, morphing from a lean young killer to a bloated wreck; far more impressive, though, is the way he shows LaMotta's brute dreams giving way to awful (and only partial) self-knowledge—you can practically see the light bulb flickering on and off over his head. The actor won an Oscar; in retrospect, and like its antihero, the film simply hit too hard to do the same.

Oscar Index · Four nominations; one win (Black-and-White Costume Design)

Original Casting · Paul Newman was considered for the role that went to Mastroianni.

How Not to Woo the Talent · Fellini tried to persuade Mastroianni to take the role by telling him "I need…a face with no personality…with no expression, a banal face—a face like yours."

How to Woo the Talent · What won Mastroianni over was Fellini's drawing of the character he wanted the actor to play. It was a sketch of a man with a giant phallus, surrounded by mermaids. Mastroianni took one look at the drawing and said: "It's an interesting part. I'll do it."

Poster Boy · After the film premiered, Fellini saw his name on a black-bordered poster tacked to the door of an Italian church. The poster read, "Let us pray for the salvation of the soul of Federico Fellini, public sinner."

6

La Dolce Vita *(1960)* It haunts our media-besotted age like a premature ghost: Nearly 40

years old, Federico Fellini's tale of a self-loathing tabloid reporter captures the glamour and hollowness of celebrity

culture with the punch of the latest scandal-induced feeding frenzy. How prescient was *La Dolce Vita*? The grumpy

little photographer who follows antihero Marcello Mastroianni around Rome is named Paparazzo; today there

are hundreds of the guys, and we call them paparazzi. ■   The film also gives us Fellini at the precise moment that he

moved from the poetic realism of *La Strada* and *Nights of Cabiria* to the increasingly whimsical fripperies of

8 1/2 and *Fellini Satyricon*. *La Dolce Vita* is grounded firmly in the day-to-day, but there are just enough scenes that lift

off into another, more dreamlike plane to give the film a larger sorrow: the celebrated opening sequence of a

statue of Christ hovering over the city, then silently moving on; the frolic with a va-va-voom starlet (Anita Ekberg) in the

Trevi Fountain; the hectic, desperate orgy in the country; the huge, rotting fish on the strand at *Vita*'s end. By that

point, Mastroianni's reporter has given up his dreams of becoming a great writer and taken a job as a publicist. Ask

anyone in the media at the turn of the millennium whether that Pilgrim's Regress doesn't sting more than ever.

The Godfather Part II

(1974) The original *Godfather* is a complete work, closed off and unimpeachable. *The Godfather Part II*, by contrast, stands as the greatest parenthesis ever put on film. By intercutting between the rise of young Vito Corleone (Robert De Niro) and the moral fall of his son Michael (Al Pacino), director Francis Ford Coppola (opposite, seated) amplified the meanings of his earlier film, daringly connecting the dots between the flawed hopes of immigrant America and the depraved sins of its corporate heirs. ■ What's most compelling about *The Godfather Part II*, though—besides cinematographer Gordon Willis' painterly shots—are the characters that parade across the canvas: Lee Strasberg's nerdy, ferocious Hyman Roth; Michael V. Gazzo's Pentangeli, the gravel-voiced turncoat; De Niro's Vito, taunting the whole notion of sequels by remaining as unknowable as Brando's. Two returning characters become figures of tragedy and vengeance: hapless Fredo (John Cazale), the runt in a litter of lions; and Kay (Diane Keaton), who finally understands how best to wound her unwoundable husband. Brooding over them all is Pacino's Michael, wielding power for his family's sake, then his business', then his own. Sixteen years later, Coppola would make the Lear analogy explicit in the lumpy, remorseful *Godfather Part III*. He didn't have to. The gutting of Michael's soul in *Part II* is awful enough. PHOTOGRAPHS BY STEVE SCHAPIRO

7

Gone With the Wind

(1939) A surpassing cinematic work of meaning and artistry? Oh, *please*. A massively engrossing four-hour soap that, all these years later, even to people who've never seen it, remains the working definition of Hollywood craft and commerce? ■ Sounds about right. ■ Many of the movies in this book are the visions of directors. *Gone With the Wind* is the work of its *producer*—and that makes all the difference. Not that David O. Selznick was a hack; he simply wanted his film to be the biggest of all time, in cultural impact and in box office dollars. And if that necessitated it also being the best, well, Selznick had the budget for it. ■ So what we have here is a women's weepie inflated to rapturously mythic proportions—Scarlett raising her fist to the sky and vowing "As God is my witness, I'll never be hungry again!"—and given real urgency by its Civil War setting and a quartet of actors who seem to have come down from Olympus to enact their parts against Selznick's opulent mural: Vivien Leigh as Scarlett, Leslie Howard as Ashley, Olivia de Havilland as Melanie, and—Jupiter himself—Clark Gable as Rhett Butler. You don't think it belongs in the top 10? Frankly, we don't give a damn.

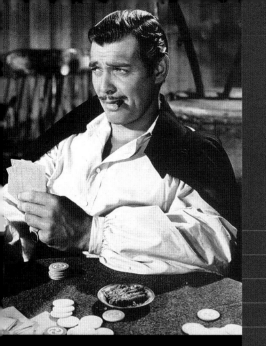

8

Oscar Index · Thirteen nominations; eight wins (including Best Picture, Best Director, Best Actress, and Best Supporting Actress)

Censor Sensibility · The folks in charge of keeping indecent material out of the movies initially balked at Rhett's immortal closing line, "Frankly, my dear, I don't give a damn." They asked that it be replaced with "Frankly, my dear, I don't give a hoot." Other alternatives said to be under consideration included "It has become of no concern to me," "My indifference is boundless," and "It makes my gorge rise."

Damned if He Does, Damned if He Doesn't · Selznick got to keep the spicy language, but it cost him a fine of $5,000.

We Knew Them When · George Reeves (who would find fame playing Superman on 1950s television) plays Brent Tarleton.

Oscar Index · Six nominations; one win (Black-and-White Costume Design)

Original Casting · Bob Hope and Danny Kaye in the lead roles; Mitzi Gaynor for the part that went to Monroe

Where They Got the Idea · A German farce, *Fanfares of Love*, about two musicians who don various disguises to get jobs.

Artistry Cannot Be Rushed · Monroe often needed more than 40 takes to get her lines right (including simple snippets of dialogue like "It's me, Sugar") even when the frustrated Wilder had them written down and hidden on the set.

Every Man's Fantasy · Curtis joked that his love scenes with Monroe were like "kissing Hitler."

Pop-Culture Obsessions · George Raft parodies his own gangster shtick (from *Scarface*) when he repeatedly tosses a coin on camera.

Some Like It Hot *(1959)* Want to get an easy laugh? Put a couple of guys in dresses. Want to make the funniest movie of all time? Have them hide out with an all-girl orchestra during a cross-country train trip, get one of them to fall so deeply in lust with a lady ukulele player that he cross-*cross*-dresses as a millionaire, and have the other one chased by *another* millionaire who won't let a simple thing like anatomy stand in the way of true love. Now keep it in the air for two hours. Then you can start calling it genius. ■ Directed by that elfin maniac Billy Wilder (left, with Jack Lemmon), from a script by Wilder and I.A.L. Diamond, *Hot* is so dazzlingly constructed that it can stand comparison to the farces of Molière and Plautus. But its greatest pleasures are contemporary: the neurotic delight Lemmon takes in becoming a skittish flapper named Daphne; Tony Curtis' deadly impersonation of Cary Grant ("Nobody talks like that!" snipes Lemmon); the odd way that this film, out of all she made, captures the carnal allure *and* the woozy sadness of Marilyn Monroe. To top it off, there's the mind-melting logic of Joe E. Brown's final line. Nobody's perfect—but this movie is.

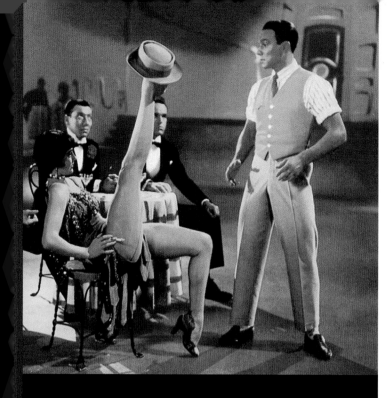

Singin' in the Rain

(1952) Why single this out of all the brilliant musicals producer Arthur Freed made during his years at MGM? Why do so many cite *Singin' in the Rain* over, say, *Meet Me In St. Louis*, *On the Town*, *An American in Paris*, *The Band Wagon*, *It's Always Fair Weather*, or *Silk Stockings*? ▪ Because, as *Casablanca* is the nonpareil example of the Hollywood machine firing on all cylinders, *Singin' in the Rain* shows what one production unit could do when songs, story, choreography, casting—*everything*—went right. Shot through with sharp Tinseltown wit, this is still one of the airiest, most confident confections you'll ever encounter. ▪ Above all, *Singin'* is artifice triumphant. Lovingly parodying the era when the arrival of talkies sowed panic in Hollywood, the plot has mellifluous bit player Debbie Reynolds giving her voice to screechy star Jean Hagen, hambone Donald O'Connor jumping through a wall that turns out to be made of paper, the gonzo film-within-a-film in which Gene Kelly does a surreal pas de deux with Cyd Charisse—and, of course, the enchanted title number. Where's the artifice in that? Kelly was suffering a cold when he shot the scene—but the smile on his face looks like transcendence itself.

Oscar Index · Two nominations; no wins

Old Tunes Never Die · The title song was originally composed by Arthur Freed and Nacio Herb Brown for another film, *The Hollywood Revue of 1929.*

Original Casting · The role of Cosmo, which eventually went to Donald O'Connor, was written with Oscar Levant in mind.

Big Break · Debbie Reynolds was 19 years old when she was cast as Gene Kelly's costar in *Singin' in the Rain*. The former Miss Burbank of 1948 had appeared in fewer than half a dozen films, all in minor roles.

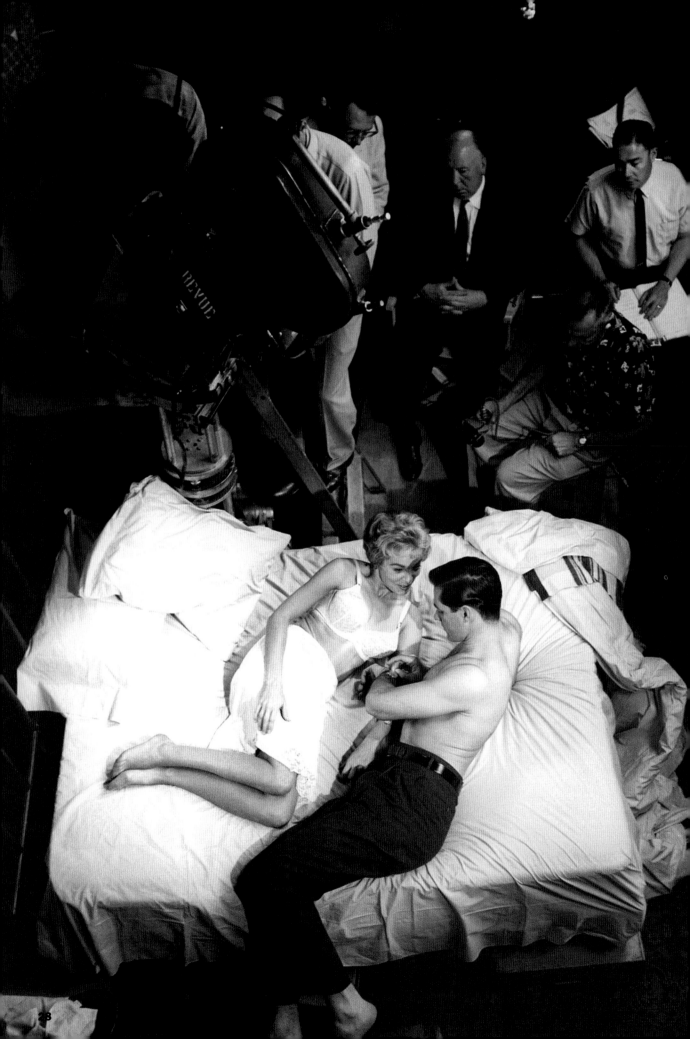

Psycho *(1960)* There's no way around it: *Psycho* cut movie history in half. When that knife came sawing past the shower curtain at poor, sheeplike Marion Crane (Janet Leigh), Alfred Hitchcock announced that from now on, all bets were off. No one was safe; a heroine could be butchered 45 minutes into the movie; a nice young hero (Anthony Perkins) could turn out to be a psychotic killer with his mama's embalmed body upstairs... ■ Oh, sorry—did we spoil the surprise? Of course not; everything about *Psycho*, from its deliberate cheapness to the harpies shrieking on the soundtrack, has been absorbed into movies in general and horror flicks in particular. To watch *Scream* or *The Texas Chainsaw Massacre* or even *The Silence of the Lambs* is to see Hitch's Rosetta stone cut to fit the latest hip attitudes, still glowing fiendishly like the skull behind Norman's face in the penultimate shot. ■ To be truthful, there's a little bit of *Psycho* in *everything* we watch nowadays. What Hitch (left, with hands folded) wrought with his little TV crew marks the demarcation, in our culture, between the age of sentiment and the age of sensation. It's to pop culture what Picasso's *Les Demoiselles d'Avignon* is to fine art: the arrival of a loud and jagged modernism. And not even *Demoiselles* made you afraid to take a shower.

Oscar Index · Four nominations; no wins

Censor Sensibility · The Production Code censors who reviewed *Psycho*'s script had no objection to the bloodletting, the oedipal murder theme, or even the shower scene—but did ask that Hitchcock remove the word *transvestite* from the film. He didn't.

Vein Glorious · The blood in the shower scene is actually chocolate syrup.

Pop-Culture Obsessions · The name of Sissy Spacek's school in *Carrie* (Bates High School) is director Brian De Palma's homage to Hitchcock and *Psycho*.

Roman à Clef Notes · Robert Bloch's novel (upon which the film is based) was inspired by the real-life story of serial killer Ed Gein, who was also the model for *The Texas Chainsaw Massacre*.

Seven Samurai *(1954)* The greatest Western

ever made. ▪ You heard us right. While Akira Kurosawa is the best known of
the Japanese directors who came to world prominence in the 1950s, even
he would have been the first to admit that he drew much of his inspiration from
Hollywood, most notably the works of John Ford. With amusing redundancy,
Hollywood chose to remake *Samurai*, six years later, as *The Magnificent Seven*,
but believe us, the original is the version you want to see. ▪ Set in the 16th
century—a chaotic, violent time in Japan's history—the film tells of a
beleaguered village whose leaders hire roving samurai to protect them from
bandits. Simple setup, astonishing dividends: Kurosawa delivers some
of the most visceral, epic action scenes ever filmed (the battle in a
driving rainstorm still amazes) while giving us the kind of complex individuals
a Hollywood writer would kill for. In particular, the wise leader of the *ronin*
(Takashi Shimura) and the crazed young samurai wannabe played by Toshiro
Mifune (right) are characters for the ages, and their relationship with
their farmer employers is depicted with a bitter humanity that sees the best
and worst in people—at the same time. Sound a little like
High Noon? Sure—but much, much higher.

Oscar Index · Two nominations; no wins

Restoration Tragedy · Kurosawa originally cut the film at 200-plus minutes,
but it was trimmed to 160 minutes for its international release.
It wasn't until 1983 that U.S. audiences got to see the full version.

Humble Beginnings · When star Toshiro Mifune returned to Japan after
service in World War II, he couldn't find a job. A friend offered to help him find
work in a film studio's photo lab. But the day he showed up, Mifune got
on the wrong line and ended up auditioning for a film role.

Getting in Touch with His Inner Warlord · Kurosawa's family was descended from
Japanese feudal nobility, and the director counted a legendary 11th-century
samurai among his ancestors.

12

The Searchers

The Searchers *(1956)* Okay, relax, here's the best *real* Western ever made—yet *The Searchers* is a movie that draws more than a bit of its greatness from context. A teenager at the turn of the millennium renting this film cold may find it a fine, tough, troubling experience, but taken as the culmination of director John Ford's and star John Wayne's careers—taken, in fact, as a harsh examination of *all* the myths and assumptions underlying Western movies—*The Searchers* remains a work of unbearable power. ■ Anyone who thinks of Wayne as a simplistic, all-American archetype would do well to watch him play Ethan Edwards, a man consumed with finding a young pioneer girl kidnapped by the Comanches on the post–Civil War prairie. As the years pass, it becomes clear that Ethan no longer wants to rescue his niece; now that she has joined the tribe (and, implicitly, slept with her captor), he just wants to kill her. He's the kind of man, Ford and Wayne acknowledge, who was crucial to "winning" the West—and also the kind of man who had to be left behind if civilization was to follow. Gorgeously shot by Winton C. Hoch, *The Searchers* is a fascinatingly curious work—the Western that casts its entire genre under suspicion.

Oscar Index · No nominations

A Jury of His Peers · Orson Welles, when asked his three favorite directors, once said, "I prefer the old masters, by which I mean John Ford, John Ford, and John Ford."

Pop-Culture Obsessions · In the film's last seconds, Wayne slowly grasps his right arm with his left hand. This was a signature shtick that costar Harry Carey had made famous in dozens of Westerns.

Indian Giver · While Ford's movies were criticized for a stereotyped portrayal of Indians, the director often shot his films in Utah's Monument Valley in part so he could pay union wages to desperately poor Navajo friends.

A Grateful Nation · The Navajo nation eventually adopted Ford into its tribe.

13

Dr. Strangelove or: How I Learned to Stop Worrying and Love the Bomb

(1964) All together now: "*We'll meet again, don't know where, don't know when...*" ▪ Such chipper words with which to send the planet off to thermonuclear Armageddon (and perhaps Stanley Kubrick—shown standing at right, with George C. Scott—is humming them himself now, in his blindingly white, climate-controlled room in heaven). And, Lord, were they a shock in 1964, when the very notion of a comedy about World War III was a slap in the face of every right-thinking citizen. Thankfully, there were enough wrong-thinking citizens around to recognize a great film when it bit them on the sensibilities. ▪ *Strangelove* rudely posits war as what big boys do to work off excess testosterone. The bombs are sent off by a demented general (Sterling Hayden) convinced that fluoridation is a Commie plot responsible for his impotency. In the war room ("You can't fight in here!"), everyone's eyes light up when they realize they'll have to procreate in the bunkers—a *lot*—to keep the human race going. And Slim Pickens orgiastically riding his "package" to earth is one of *Strangelove*'s most felicitous touches. (Peter Sellers, in three roles—sane, less sane, *insane*—is another.) How much safer, in every sense, is the world today? Enough that this movie would never—and *could* never—be made.

Oscar Index · Four nominations; no wins

Where They Got the idea · Kubrick based his film on Peter George's 1958 novel *Red Alert*, a serious story of accidental nuclear war.

Fine-tuning the Concept · Kubrick soon realized a movie about something as unthinkable as nuclear war had to be "a black comedy, or better, a nightmare comedy."

What Did They Know? · *The New York Times*' critic described the film as "grave and dangerous . . . the most shattering sick joke I've ever come across."

The Game of the Name · One of the three characters Sellers portrays is President Merkin Muffley. *Merkin* is the name for a pubic-hair wig.

14

The Gold Rush *(1925)* We confess to something of a bias. The Charlie Chaplin films that invariably land on lists like these are the more consciously poetic works of the 1930s: *City Lights* (1931) and *Modern Times* (1936). They're wonderful; by all means, don't miss them. That said, the Chaplin that simply makes us laugh hardest, without falling into sticky conceits of universal "little men," is *The Gold Rush.* ■ If you doubt that Chaplin was a stone master of physical comedy, watch the celebrated business with the shoe here. Gold prospector Charlie's up in the Klondike, stuck in a cabin, out of food. He boils his boot and begins eating as if this were a French restaurant and he'd just been served the capon: twiddling the laces on a fork, picking his teeth with the nails. Then there are larger wonders, like the cabin's dance on the cliff edge; some sighing over a dance-hall girl (Georgia Hale) who's allowed to be a bit tougher than the usual Charlie darling; and a historical long view—those masses of men in the snow—that gives *Gold Rush* its surprising emotional spine. Was Chaplin the greatest comic mind of our century? Watch this and discuss—once your sides have stopped hurting.

Oscar Index · First release predates the Academy Awards; upon rerelease in 1942, *The Gold Rush* was nominated in the two categories in which it was eligible—sound and score—but won neither award.

Recalled to Life · When Chaplin reportedly screened *The Gold Rush* for his children and their friends, narrating the story himself, it was such a hit with the family that he decided to rerelease the film, with a new musical score and his own narration in place of the old dialogue cards.

Where They Got the Idea · Chaplin's premise was inspired, in part, by the Donner Party—a group of pioneers, many of whom starved to death in the snow while on a cross-country expedition in the 1840s.

15

Star Wars *(1977)* Think of movies as little planets of narrative. The first ones were mere space dust: some guy sneezing in Thomas Edison's lab. With *Star Wars*, George Lucas delivered unto us a galaxy. ■ No one is denying that the plot and characters rehash adventure-tale clichés from Arthurian quests to comic-book mythologies (call them "archetypes" if you're pompously inclined). What matters is the visualization and conviction of the thing: the swagger of Harrison Ford's Han Solo, the gleaming evil of Darth Vader, the gut wrench of the leap into hyperspace, the twittering delight of the cantina scene, the growth of a callow kid named Luke Skywalker. And on and on. To those who saw this stuff in their youth, *Star Wars* understandably became the cornerstone of entire moviegoing lives. ■ As these words are written, the first film in the next *Star Wars* trilogy is upon us; clearly, Lucas wants to give us the universe now. With the Web in full cry, the media kneeling at the director's sneaker-clad feet, and the faithful camping out at ticket windows, *Star Wars: Episode I—The Phantom Menace* has already become one of the biggest events in movie history. Still, it's only reflecting the light of that original galaxy far, far away.

16

Oscar Index · Ten nominations; six wins (including Original Score and Film Editing)

Overweening Ambition · Lucas at first envisioned packing into one movie all of the events and characters that later became the *Star Wars* trilogy.

Original Title · The working title of the script's first draft was *The Adventures of the Starkiller*.

Fine-tuning the Concept · Lucas considered casting the part that became Obi-Wan Kenobi with a Japanese actor.

Pop-Culture Obsessions · Lucas was inspired, in part, by Akira Kurosawa's *The Hidden Fortress*, a 1958 adventure in which a princess is escorted to freedom by two bickering peasants—who became the droids in *Star Wars*.

What Did They Know? · *The New Republic* said of *Star Wars*: "The dialogue...sticks in the actors' mouths like peanut butter.... Its visual imagination and special effects...are unexceptional."

On the Waterfront

(1954) Burdened by parody (how many impressionists have urgently muttered, "Chah-lie...I coulda been a contendah"?), hobbled by suspicions that it served as a rat's rationale for director Elia Kazan, *Waterfront* is nevertheless the most beautifully crafted of 1950s message movies. It was also a tough shoot: an anticorruption tale that filmed on the Mob-infested docks of Hoboken, N.J., with boxers cast as union goons, longshoremen picking up day work as extras, and police protection for the cast and crew. ■ Out of all the crosscurrents—not least among them, hostility over Kazan's friendly testimony before the House Un-American Activities Committee—came a startlingly poetic film. Terry Malloy remains one of Marlon Brando's most incandescent roles: a thug who slowly comes to his senses—and then stumbles toward a greater nobility—when he sees what racketeers have done to his life, friends, and family. There were plenty of movies made about the working class at this time, but because of Brando, and Eva Marie Saint as his slowly bending love, *Waterfront* is one of the very few that doesn't feel condescending. On the contrary, it blows away the stench of its subject—not to mention the cloud around its maker—on a deeply humane breeze.

Oscar Index · Twelve nominations; eight wins (including Best Picture, Best Director, Best Actor, and Best Supporting Actress)

Original Casting · Frank Sinatra in the role of Terry Malloy, which eventually went to Brando

Conditional Casting · Brando agreed to take the role only if he could leave the Hoboken set every day at 4 p.m. to drive across the Hudson River and meet with his psychoanalyst in Manhattan.

The Natives Were Restless · Actual Hoboken longshoremen were cast as extras and paid the same wages they earned for dock work. When their payroll was once late in arriving, two longshoremen grabbed assistant director Charlie Maguire and held him over the water, off the side of a pier, demanding their money.

As It Happened · One of the film's most famous scenes (in which Eva Marie Saint drops her glove and Brando picks it up, then puts it on his own hand) was unplanned: Saint dropped the glove accidentally and Brando improvised the rest.

17

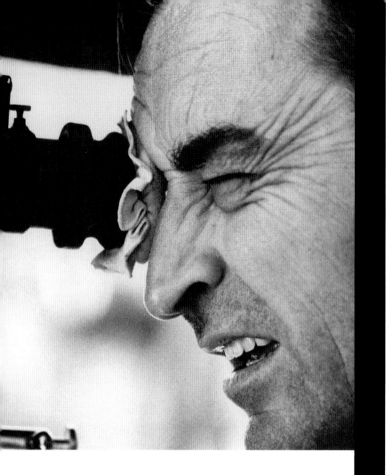

Lawrence of Arabia (1962)

A massive, stirring war epic at the center of which is...a blur. Remember the scene where T.E. Lawrence (Peter O'Toole) emerges from the desert heat waves, carrying a fallen Arab on his shoulders? That's a handy image: In all the film's 200-plus minutes, Lawrence never becomes more than a charismatic mirage. As such, he was the perfect hero for a moviegoing age that didn't really trust them. ■ The opacity was deliberate on the part of director David Lean (left), who was fascinated by the way the real-life Lawrence obliterated his Englishness to help lead Arab nations to independence during WWI. Lean could only imply his protagonist's tortured homosexuality (and even those hints were edited out of many release prints), but the casting of blue-eyed O'Toole—so dashing, so unsure—got the point across. *Lawrence of Arabia* is a mighty thing to behold on a big screen: Maurice Jarre's heaving music; growling performances from Omar Sharif and Anthony Quinn (opposite, top); the bloody onrush of the raid on Aqaba; all that endless, sensuous *sand*. But amid the pageantry is the distressingly modern sight of a man crossing a desert to lose himself—and, to his terror, finding himself a legend instead.

Oscar Index · Ten nominations; seven wins (including Best Picture and Film Editing)

How It All Began · Lean and producer Sam Spiegel were looking for an epic to follow *The Bridge on the River Kwai*. They considered a Gandhi biopic, but, according to Lean, the pragmatic Spiegel "didn't think a picture about an Indian would be box office."

Original Casting · The lead was offered to Marlon Brando, Anthony Perkins, and Albert Finney.

What Did They Know? · *The New York Times* said of *Lawrence*, "It is, in the last analysis, just a huge, thundering camel opera that tends to run down rather badly as it rolls on into its third hour...."

Producer's Cut · Lean claimed that Spiegel went behind his back and trimmed the original 3-hour, 40-minute version of *Lawrence* (in response to theater owners' complaints that it was too long to be commercial) without his knowledge.

18

Vertigo *(1958)* The closest that Alfred Hitchcock ever came to a personal statement, and you'd better believe it's disturbing. The plot reads like a case history: Acrophobic detective Jimmy Stewart falls for an acquaintance's wife (Kim Novak), torments himself with guilt when she dies, then flips out when he meets her down-market double (Novak again). There's a murder mystery in here somewhere, but it's beside the point. What Hitch is after is how selfless love can turn into self-absorbed obsession. When Stewart meets Novak 2.0, he transforms her into the image of his dead beloved—dying her hair blond, buying her the same clothes, fretting over every nuance of her presentation. In short, he's a grieving monster, and Stewart, in the performance of his career, lets us see the sad, lost Jimmy of an earlier era behind the delusions.

■ Filmed like a fever dream, blessed with Bernard Herrmann's most rhapsodic score, *Vertigo* isn't much "fun" in the playful Hitchcockian manner of *North by Northwest*. How could it be, when Stewart's search for the blond ice maiden of his psyche so closely mirrors the director's? The movie ends, fittingly, with a nun, for— make no mistake—this is a confession.

JAMES STEWART
KIM NOVAK
IN ALFRED HITCHCOCK'S
MASTERPIECE

'VERTIGO'

19

Oscar Index · Nine nominations; four wins (including Visual Effects)

Original Titles · *Growing Up*, *A Boy's Life*, and *E.T. and Me*

Creature Features · Three separate E.T.'s (costing $1.5 million) were used in the film: an electronic version for detailed facial expressions, a mechanical version that moved its limbs, and a "live" model, used for walking, that was variously inhabited by several dwarfs and a little boy who had no legs. This model once caught fire with one of the dwarfs inside.

Vocal Yokel · E.T.'s voice was supplied in part by actress Debra Winger and in part by a Marin County, Calif., housewife in her 60s whom the producers coaxed into speaking without her dentures.

Product Displacement · The script originally called for E.T. to take a shine to M&M's, but Mars didn't want to be involved with the film. Hershey, however, agreed to allow Reese's Pieces to be used in the film, and sales of the candy tripled within two weeks of *E.T.*'s release.

Huh? · Ted Koppel said of *E.T.*: "It is essentially the Christ story. Christ was the ultimate extraterrestrial."

E.T. The Extra-Terrestrial (1982) Despite the

honor and acclaim that have accrued to Steven Spielberg for
Schindler's List and *Saving Private Ryan*—despite the pains he takes
to assure us he's all grown up now—the film that still feels closest
to the man is the one where an alien comes to suburbia and befriends
a lonely little boy. ▪ The enchantment of *E.T.* lies in its unapologetic
use of fantasy to soothe emotional wounds. What child of divorce
wouldn't want a pint-size pal from outer space to squirrel away in the
back of his closet—especially when that pal is so clearly lost himself?
"Phone home" is E.T.'s plaintive mantra, but it's also Spielberg's
reminder that we ignore our families at our peril. The director took his
child's-eye view seriously, rarely moving the camera higher than
star Henry Thomas' height. The result is a film that precisely captures
the material comforts and dreadful uncertainties of an average
American middle-class kid. *E.T.*'s a beautiful dream, of course—
we can only hope our bicycles will fly us away from it all—
but it's a film made by a man who clearly remembers what it
was like to be an alien in suburbia.

47

Oscar Index · 14 nominations; 6 wins (including Best Picture)

Original Casting · Claudette Colbert for Margo until a ruptured disk forced her to drop out. She later said, "Every time I read the beautiful notices, a knife goes through my heart."

Sense of Direction · Mankiewicz on how to play Margo: "She is a woman who treats a mink coat like a poncho."

Roman à Clef Notes · Davis and on-screen lover Gary Merrill became an item during filming, marrying not long after the wrap.

Film Comment · Holm on Monroe: "I thought she was quite sweet and terribly dumb, and my natural reaction was 'Whose girl is that?'"

All About Eve

(1950) There are Eve Harringtons in every walk of life—their limpid, gentle smiles a cover for carnivorous ambition—but how wonderful that *All About Eve* finds her on Broadway, in a milieu where no one is not an actor and everyone is suspect. Bette Davis reclaimed her Hollywood crown as waspish, neurotic star Margo Channing —the only character certain from the beginning that ingenue Eve (Anne Baxter) is out for blood—but everybody's a charmer in writer-director Joseph L. Mankiewicz's acid valentine to the stage, from adorably nasty George Sanders to gossipy, wise Celeste Holm to a dewy-eyed ingenue with ambitions of her own: Miss Marilyn Monroe.

21

22

Oscar Index · No nominations

Serendipitous Casting · Maggiorani was a real-life steel factory worker; Staiola was discovered in a crowd watching the shooting of *The Bicycle Thief*.

Neoreality Check · Afterward, Maggiorani went back to the factory, where his new wealth and fame made him a tad unpopular.

Neoreality Bites · Maggiorani soon found himself unemployed.

...And Mickey Rooney Would Play the Boy · David O. Selznick offered to back the film— if Cary Grant could play the father.

The Bicycle Thief

(1948) Every artistic medium, if it wants to stay alive, needs to go back to basics every so often. Think punk rock, think French Impressionism, think *The Bicycle Thief*. Vittorio De Sica's disarmingly simple story of a poor man's search for the stolen bike he needs so desperately for a job captures the postwar streets of Rome with a bleak fidelity that still stings. The most beloved film in the Italian neorealist movement, *Thief* is heartbreaking in its depiction of the shifting relationship between a caring father (Lamberto Maggiorani) and the young son (Enzo Staiola) who slowly becomes his dad's consoler.

Snow White and the Seven Dwarfs

(1937) Pinocchio may represent the high point of his animation wizardry, *Fantasia* may flaunt his artistic ambitions more blatantly—but *Snow White* is the film that made Walt Disney a Hollywood player, proved that "feature-length cartoon" wasn't an oxymoron, and most simply and elegantly retains the Magic that today feels so corporatized. Like all the best fairy tales, it's both dreamlike and terrifying (the scene where the queen turns into a hag can make a jaded adult feel like a frightened little kid again), but Disney's pop genius is most evident in the transformation of seven random dwarfs into Grumpy, Happy, Dopey, et al. Whistle while you watch it.

23

Oscar Index · One nomination; no wins

Milestones · *Snow White* was the first American feature-length cartoon.

The Game of the Name · Trial monikers for the seven dwarfs included Hoppy, Scrappy, Crabby, Blabby, Hotsy, Shifty, Awful, Biggy-Wiggy, and Neurtsy.

Cooler Heads Prevailed · Some of Disney's crew worried that the name Dopey would suggest that the dwarf was indulging in, uh, recreational substances.

Ah-choo! · Comedian Billy Gilbert had to audition one of his trademark sneezes for Walt before being cast as Sneezy.

What Did They Know? · During production, Hollywood skeptics called *Snow White* "Disney's Folly."

Champion In the Making · A young dancer named Marjorie Belcher was the animators' model for Snow White. She later became known as Marge Champion, dance partner and wife of Gower.

Oscar Index · No nominations

Roman à Clef Notes · Co-screenwriter Dudley Nichols based the madcap romance on Hepburn's affair with director John Ford at the time.

Inspiration · Hawks modeled Grant's character, David, on silent-film comedian Harold Lloyd.

They Thought It Meant "Happy" · Censors fussed about using the names of real-life politicians Al Smith and Jim Farley (which were changed to Mickey-the-Mouse and Donald-the-Duck), but ignored Grant's line about going "gay."

Dog Star · Skippy the terrier (George) also played Asta in *The Thin Man* and Mr. Smith in *The Awful Truth*.

Bringing Up Baby *(1938)* There are great screwball comedies—and then there's the one that actually pushes the envelope of sanity. *Baby* playfully throws all sorts of goonery into its mix: two leopards (one tame, one not so), the intercostal clavicle of a brontosaurus, a yappy little dog that likes bones, and so forth. But its most unnerving, enduring pleasure is in watching Cary Grant's patented aplomb destroyed by a magnificently eccentric Katharine Hepburn. Directed by Howard Hawks with all the throttles open, *Baby* is demented enough to drive some viewers crazy—but it finds a midsummer night's soul in Hepburn's unearthly, burbling laugh.

24

25

Intolerance *(1916)* Out of the cradle, endlessly rocking... *The Birth of a Nation* is usually cited as D.W. Griffith's crowning achievement, but the director's massively ambitious feature-film follow-up now looks to be the greater movie—and not just because it lacks the virulently rosy racism that has always crippled *Birth*. Shifting between a modern morality tale, the massacre of Huguenots in 16th-century France, the life and death of Christ, and—with a visual opulence beyond belief—the fall of Babylon, Griffith displays his mastery of narrative and character, and works up to an orgy of crosscutting in which sheer moviemaking bravura transcends the inherent corn.

Oscar Index · Predated the Academy Awards

How They Did It · The spectacular crane shot that introduces Belshazzar's feast was achieved by placing a camera on an elevator mounted on a railroad flatcar. As the elevator descended, the flatcar was moved forward.

Net Gain · Extras earned $2.50 a day—plus an extra $5 if they would leap from sets more than 100 feet high into off-camera nets during battle scenes.

Prop Department · The Babylonian extras' beards (made of crepe paper and wire) doubled as sun visors during breaks.

2001: A Space Odyssey (1968) Stanley Kubrick's

trip movie par excellence blew as many movie conventions as
it did minds: No longer did a film have to make sense to make, like,
sense. *2001*'s absurdly ambitious time frame stretches from
our ape forebears to the evolved Starchild who floats to Earth at the
end; in between, two wayward spacemen struggle with a computer,
the silken-voiced HAL 9000, that outclasses them in brains, heart,
and insecurity. A chilly bulletin from the cinema of the future,
2001 is a heaven-sent vision—and a hell of a ride.

the ultimate trip

26

2001: A SPACE ODYSSEY

Oscar Index · Four nominations; one win (Special Effects)

The Game of the Name · HAL is an acronym from the words *heuristic* and *algorithmic*.

"Daisy, Daisy..." · Actors Nigel Davenport, Martin Balsam, and Douglas Rain recorded HAL's voice, but only Rain had the right stuff.

Prop Department · The dead zebra in the Dawn of Man section was a dead horse painted with stripes. It reeked so horrendously that the leopard was loath to go near its cast mate.

What Did They Know? · Critic Pauline Kael called *2001* "a monumentally unimaginative movie."

Like, Wow... · Kubrick on the psychedelic Star Gate sequence: "I have to say, it was never meant to represent an acid trip."

The Grapes of Wrath

(1940) A movie that made no bones about who the villains of the Great Depression were—the bankers, the big farm interests—by definition had powerful people trying hard to keep it unmade. To that end, filming proceeded under heavy security. Yet, 60 years later, in an America fat with success, this adaptation of the John Steinbeck novel still plays with a brave and uncommon power. Henry Fonda's simmering portrayal of Okie Tom Joad made him a top star, and the camera work has the steadfast truth of a Walker Evans photograph— but it is director John Ford who makes this dust-bowl stations of the cross so harsh and so enduring.

27

Pulp Fiction *(1994)* He may never make another film as good, but Quentin Tarantino's sly, gutbucket modern noir will long be savored by fans of trash rock, retro-razor-blade dialogue, and plain old great filmmaking. Careening through three tales of the criminal demimonde, *Pulp* plays with time, veers off on lunatic tangents, gives performers like John Travolta, Uma Thurman, and Christopher Walken real meat to bite into, and—in Samuel L. Jackson's heroic final monologue—locates a weary, hard-won moralism. Don't blame Tarantino for the *Pulp* wannabes that followed: This one is the Grand Royale.

Oscar Index · 11 nominations; 3 wins (including Original Screenplay)

Roman à Clef Notes · Montgomery Clift passed on the Holden role—possibly because it too closely paralleled his affair with 49-year-old singer Libby Holman.

Inside Joke · When Swanson says the line "We had faces," she is watching herself in 1928's *Queen Kelly*, a financial disaster directed by Erich von Stroheim (who plays Max).

Driven Performance · Though cast as the chauffeur, Von Stroheim didn't know how to drive.

Sunset Boulevard

(1950) "Mr. DeMille, I'm ready for my close-up..." But do you really think Hollywood was ready for this maggoty, microscopic examination of the way the film industry eats its elders? On the contrary, an enraged Louis B. Mayer bellowed to Billy Wilder at an industry screening that the director should be tarred, feathered, and run out of Hollywood. Like a cruel mirror, *Sunset* casts aging silent-film star Gloria Swanson as aging silent-film star Norma Desmond, William Holden as a hack screenwriter-turned-gigolo, and a spook's gallery of bona fide has-beens. It's Wilder's blackest joke—and probably the only movie to feature a funeral for a pet chimp.

Oscar Index · Seven nominations; one win (Original Screenplay)

He Got Game · At their first meeting, Tarantino made Travolta play board games based on *Grease*, *Welcome Back, Kotter*, and *Saturday Night Fever*.

Glad It Didn't Work Out · Tarantino wanted to score the sodomy scene with the Knack's "My Sharona," but couldn't get the rights.

Just Imagine If It Had Been in 3-D · A diabetic viewer fainted following the hypo-in-the-heart scene.

The Maltese Falcon

(1941) Howard Hawks' *The Big Sleep* may be more fetchingly baroque, but director John Huston's debut, adapted from Dashiell Hammett's novel, is still the genre's ground zero—a template for all gumshoe flicks to come. *Falcon*'s casting is uncanny: Each actor is the exact visual correlative of his or her pulp "type." A fey henchman could *only* be Peter Lorre, or a doomed gunman Elisha Cook Jr., or a duplicitous babe Mary Astor. And a brutally competent, morally exhausted, trenchantly sexy private eye named Sam Spade could be nobody but Bogart.

31

Mr. Smith Goes to Washington

(1939) Regardless of whether you think Frank Capra's little-guy-against-the-Senate populism is dangerously naive or right on the money, there's no denying the way *Mr. Smith* thrillingly plays to all our ideals; in the wake of recent scandals, this film seems both further away and more beguilingly of the moment than ever. And Jimmy Stewart, in the role that made him a star, is astounding. From the hush of the Lincoln Memorial scenes to the raspy, betrayed despair of the final filibuster, his performance shows an actor coming into the full power of his craft—and then hiding it.

30

Oscar Index · Ten nominations; one win (Original Story)

How He Did It · To achieve appropriate hoarseness for the famous filibuster speech, Stewart inflamed his throat with dichloride of mercury.

Cause Célèbre · Shocked by the depiction of Senate graft and National Press Club tippling, a third of the politico-packed audience walked out of *Mr. Smith*'s Washington premiere.

Mr. Smith Almost Didn't Go to Washington · Hoping to appease the politicos, rival studios offered Columbia $2 million to shelve the film.

Oscar Index · Three nominations; no wins

Who Dunnit? · Bogie, not Huston, came up with the famous "stuff that dreams are made of" line (with a nod to William Shakespeare).

The *Real* Stuff That Dreams Are Made Of · The six prop falcons were constructed of hollow plaster and black enamel paint, and cost $114 each.

The Wizard of Oz *(1939)* For anyone who came of age watching Dorothy try to get home every year on TV, *The Wizard of Oz* is an intensely private and secretly shared myth. Drop a line at any cocktail party—"Pay no attention to that man behind the curtain," or "Toto, too?"—and faces will glow with remembered pleasures. Scorned by critics in 1939, *Wizard* still hits home with children through its dreamy Technicolor opulence, its terrifying witch, and the fairy-tale camaraderie between a scarecrow (Ray Bolger), a tin man (Jack Haley), a lion (Bert Lahr), and an achingly wistful little girl (Judy Garland, who never did make it over the rainbow).

32

33

Jules and Jim *(1961)* François Truffaut's most beloved film tells of a lovers' triangle before, during, and after WWI—and mirrors the world's larger disillusionment in the crack-up of a privileged ménage à trois. Oskar Werner and Henri Serre are the two idealistic young men and the unforgettable Jeanne Moreau is Catherine, the free spirit they share even as her bewitching impulsiveness turns increasingly manic. Based on the novel by Henri-Pierre Roché, whose later (and more clearly autobiographical) book, *Two English Girls*, was turned by Truffaut into a brilliantly dark 1972 double to the earlier film, *Jules* is a paean to the beautiful follies of youth— and the crest of the French New Wave.

Oscar Index · No nominations

His Stomach Felt Like *Duck Soup* · The night of the film's French premiere, Truffaut was so nervous he opted for a Marx Brothers movie instead of his own.

Censor Sensibility · *Jules and Jim*'s casual depiction of adultery earned it the French equivalent of an X rating and the wrath of French family groups who wanted the film banned.

Keep an Eye Peeled · Because Truffaut didn't want his characters to age physically over the more-than-20-year period of the film, he subtly used Picasso paintings from the master's different periods to reflect time's passage.

34

Sherlock Jr. *(1924) The General* is the Buster Keaton film that usually lands on lists like these, but, as wondrous as it is, we'll take *Sherlock Jr.* anytime. The timid projectionist who dreams his way into the movie he's showing is Keaton at his most astoundingly typical: clever, heartstoppingly graceful, and playfully philosophic about the medium he made his own. For a "How'd he do that?" thrill, watch the long-shot scene in which Buster jumps through a window and emerges on the other side disguised as an old woman. Better, for a gentle discourse on cinema itself, watch the projectionist jump onto his screen—and suffer the slings and arrows of outrageous cross-cutting.

8½ *(1963)* Navel gazing was never so brilliant: For his eighth-and-a-half film ("half" counts work on two omnibus flicks), Federico Fellini (opposite, with Claudia Cardinale) gave us a self-pitying director (Marcello Mastroianni) who flees a cacophony of lovers, movie people, and circus performers for his own psychic nether regions. Self-indulgent? Yup. Brutally honest and strangely moving? All of that, and more. Nino Rota's score is positively giddy, and Gianni Di Venanzo's cinematography, a feast—but most memorable is the paradox of a brilliantly imagined film about...creative block.

Oscar Index · Six nominations; two wins (Best Actor, Adapted Screenplay)

Original Casting · MGM wanted Joan Crawford until it discovered that Hepburn and Howard Hughes owned the rights to Philip Barry's play.

Wordsmith · Donald Ogden Stewart on his script: It "was the easiest Oscar that you could imagine. All I had to do was get out of the way."

A Sense of Direction · When Jimmy Stewart was having trouble with his "hearth fires and holocausts" speech, Cukor had visitor Noël Coward remark on how "devastating" he was in the part. Flattered, he did the scene without a hitch.

The Philadelphia Story

(1940) Oh, how the rich do play. With characters like Tracy Lord, Macaulay Connor, and C.K. Dexter Haven, even the *names* are elegant in George Cukor's deeply pleasing adaptation of the Philip Barry stage comedy. Katharine Hepburn reignited her stalled movie career by cannily playing a part close to the public's perception of her: Tracy is an upper-class ice maiden who melts, with blissful unease, when confronted with her own callousness. Or with Oscar winner Jimmy Stewart in a bathrobe. Or both. Cary Grant, meanwhile, gets to toss off lines like "No mean Machiavelli is smiling, cynical Sidney Kidd." My, it's yar.

3 5

3 6

Oscar Index · Five nominations; one win (Foreign Film)

Original Casting · Unbelievably, Fellini once imagined Laurence Olivier in the role that went to Mastroianni.

Roman à Clef Notes · A year before starting 8 1/2, Fellini visited a Jungian analyst and began recording his dreams.

Art Imitates Life · Unable to finish his script, Fellini had an epiphany: He "would make [the film] the story of a director who no longer knew what he wanted to make."

Emetic Acting · For one of her scenes, Sandra Milo spent a day consuming, then vomiting, 16 chicken legs.

Jungian Analysis · After dozing through 8 1/2, Khrushchev okayed its Soviet release, saying a "film that gives me two hours...sleep in the middle of Moscow can't be dangerous."

Blue Velvet (1986) Andy Hardy, meet

Salvador Dalí. ■ Quite possibly the most subversive film
ever released into commercial theaters, *Velvet* remains
writer-director David Lynch's personal best: a film that
crawls beneath America's well-manicured lawn to find the
insects burrowing out of our ids. Kyle MacLachlan is
the Tom Swiftian hero, drawn ineluctably to the bad side of
town and the closet of tortured chanteuse Isabella
Rossellini, while Dennis Hopper plays the most evil man in
the history of film. If movies are a culturally sanctioned
form of dreaming, then this is the nightmare that's always
hovering out there on the fringes, ready to erupt.

Oscar Index · Five nominations;
one win (Song)

Original Casting · Robert Duvall
(Haven Hamilton), Susan Anspach
(Barbara Jean)

Wordsmiths · First-time actress
Blakley wrote her breakdown
monologue. Ditto: Barbara Baxley and
Geraldine Chaplin, who improvised
most of their dialogue.

How They Did It · A specially developed
eight-track system was used to get
Nashville's distinctive aural texture.

What Did He Know? · Mooney Lynn
(husband of Loretta, assumed model
for Barbara Jean) on *Nashville*: "It was
the worst goddamn movie I ever saw."

38

37

Oscar Index · One nomination; no wins

Inspiration · Bobby Vinton's version of "Blue Velvet."
According to Lynch, "There was something
mysterious about it. It made me think about things."

But... · He wrote the script while listening to Dmitri
Shostakovich's Symphony No. 15 in A.

Serendipity · Lynch got the idea to use Roy Orbison's
"In Dreams" after hearing "Crying" while riding in a taxi.

In Dreams, Indeed · The ending came to Lynch in a dream.

Hmmmm... · In a bid for the role of sex-crazed,
gas-sniffing, woman-beating Frank,
Dennis Hopper told Lynch, "I am Frank."

Nashville *(1975)* Robert Altman's films always teem with messy, fascinating life—and none more so than this one, which seems to hold in its 159 minutes all the deluded, desperate, idealistic currents of post-'60s America. Following 24 characters as they wend their way through the title city, converging on a concert–cum–political rally at which everything comes to a head, *Nashville* manages to interweave the country's cultural disillusions with more personal betrayals. For all the funk, it's compulsively watchable, with rich performances by Lily Tomlin, Barbara Harris, Ned Beatty, Keith Carradine, Ronee Blakley, and a C&W soundtrack that sounds like the real thing—but bites a lot harder.

Swing Time *(1936) Top Hat* often gets the nod for its wiggy Art Deco dreamscapes, but *Swing Time* is the best of the 10 musicals starring Fred Astaire and Ginger Rogers—the one where they seem the most like equals dancing with the idea of love, and less like brilliant hoofers crammed into a fine, but stilted, romance. In other words, *Swing Time* feels like it catches the *real* Astaire and Rogers: two pros who mildly resented the public's demand for their pairing yet gave it all they had. The musical numbers, needless to say, are sublime, from the pep of "Pick Yourself Up" to the braggadocio of "Bojangles of Harlem" to the gossamer simplicity of the Oscar-winning "The Way You Look Tonight." Topping them all is the elegantly wise "Never Gonna Dance," in which Fred and Ginger disprove the title even as they enact it.

39

Oscar Index · Twelve nominations; seven wins (including Best Picture)

Auteur Trepidation · Oscar winner Spielberg initially feared that he wasn't up to the subject and offered *Schindler* to Holocaust survivor Roman Polanski, then to Martin Scorsese.

Character Notes · Spielberg's model for Schindler was mogul Steve Ross.

How They Did It · A handheld camera was used for 40 percent of the movie to give it a documentary feel.

40

Schindler's List *(1993)* Steven Spielberg had to come of age someday, and this film carries both the awful weight of history and a more private sense of reckoning. By giving us the Holocaust through the eyes of an outsider—a cynical German industrialist (Liam Neeson) who only slowly comes to accept his mission as savior—*List* exerted a universal appeal. Ironically, though, what makes the film live on as a cultural monument *and* a great movie is the way Spielberg hid most of his cinematic bag of tricks behind a simple, black-and-white presentation of events. PHOTOGRAPHS BY DAVID JAMES

41

Taxi Driver *(1976)* Before the heart of New York City was a Disney-fied tourist heaven, children, it was hell. And no film plumbed this city's depths with more aghast, color-saturated empathy than Martin Scorsese's tale of a despairing cabbie and his collision with the world. *Taxi Driver* catches all the paranoia of its times and then some, with Robert De Niro frighteningly real as the wannabe assassin, director Scorsese (above, left) spewing bile from the backseat, and Jodie Foster hard and innocent as a preteen hooker. The reason we still nervously joke about that scene where De Niro growls "You talkin' to *me*?" is because the movie so fiendishly did.

PHOTOGRAPHS BY STEVE SCHAPIRO

Oscar Index · Four nominations; no wins

As It Happened · The famous "You talkin' to *me*?" sequence was improvised in front of the camera.

Where They Got the Idea · The diary of Arthur Bremer, who shot Alabama governor (and presidential candidate) George Wallace in 1972, partly inspired screenwriter Paul Schrader—who has described himself as having been "enamored of guns...drinking heavily...[and] obsessed with pornography."

Life Imitates Art · Before the 1981 assassination attempt on President Reagan, Schrader got a letter from one "J.W. Hinckley" asking to meet Foster. Schrader thought the letter was from a "smitten groupie" and threw it away.

Oscar Index · Seven nominations; two wins (Visual Effects and Sound Effects Editing)

Delusions of Grandeur · Cameron has described *Aliens* as an allegory for American involvement in Vietnam, with "high-tech soldiers [pitted] against an unseen, wraithlike enemy."

Multiplicity · While Cameron was writing *Aliens*, he was also working on *The Terminator* and penning a draft of *Rambo: First Blood Part II*. He used a different desk for each project and would also put on different music whenever he sat down to write one of the films.

Oscar Index · No nominations

Marxist Economics · After *Duck Soup* flopped, the Marx Brothers left Paramount and went to MGM, where they made one of their biggest hits, *A Night at the Opera*.

Soup to Nuts · When the mayor of Fredonia, N.Y., protested the use of his municipality's moniker, Groucho responded: "Change the name of your town. It is hurting our picture."

What Did They Know? · *The Nation*: "Pretty near everyone seems to have agreed that...the Four Marx Brothers are not quite so amusing."

Aliens *(1986)* The finest pure action movie ever made? Hard to argue, when director James Cameron kicks the extraterrestrial dread of Ridley Scott's 1979 *Alien* into overdrive—and keeps it there for 137 sense-stunning minutes. But the hectic terror that ensues when space Marines land on a planet populated by...*them* would be one empty exercise if not for the bond between Ripley (Sigourney Weaver, going Rambo with a vengeance) and a little girl named Newt (Carrie Henn). When Ripley protects her charge from Mama alien by bellowing "Get away from her, you *bitch*!" audiences roar—in approval *and* release.

43

42

Duck Soup *(1933)* Hail, Freedonia! Nobody wanted political satire in 1933—especially the blistering buffoonery on display here. Thus the Marx Brothers' *Duck Soup* was a commercial flop, but after its rediscovery by college students in the anarchic 1960s, the movie now looks to be a classic of aggressive nonsense. Wielding puns as if they were lances, Groucho plays Rufus T. Firefly, leader of a tin-pot republic; dimly insistent Chico and mute gremlin Harpo are a combination spy/peanut vendor/chauffeur outfit. (Zeppo, as always, plays...Zeppo.) The scene where Groucho sings, "If you think this country's bad off now/Just wait'll I get through with it!" may be the truest bit of politics ever put on film.

44

North by Northwest *(1959)* The master's greatest toy is a Rube Goldberg contraption with moral underpinnings. Cary Grant has the quintessential I'm-having-one-of-those-*days* Hitchcock role as a Manhattan businessman who gets mistaken for a spy, framed for murder at the U.N., chased by a biplane in the middle of a cornfield, and wooed by an ambiguous beauty (Eva Marie Saint). That Grant ends up hanging off Mount Rushmore is simply Hitchcockian felicity; more important is the way he evolves from an aimless suit in thrall to his own mum to a caring, feeling man. Even if he isn't quite sure *which* man that is.

Oscar Index · Three nominations; no wins

How It All Began · Hitchcock mentioned in a development meeting that he had always wanted to do a chase sequence across the faces of Mount Rushmore.

How They Did It · The U.S. Government would not allow any violent scenes to be filmed at Mount Rushmore, which forced Hitchcock to shoot inside a studio with oversize sets, backdrops, and photographic plates of the monument.

Original Casting · Jimmy Stewart lobbied unsuccessfully for Cary Grant's part and MGM wanted Cyd Charisse for the role that went to Eva Marie Saint.

Oops! · In the scene where Saint shoots Grant in the cafeteria at Mount Rushmore, a little boy can be seen covering his ears a few seconds before her gun goes off.

Original Titles · The in-progress script was variously called *Breathless*, *In a Northwesterly Direction*, and (tongue-in-cheek) *The Man on Lincoln's Nose*.

The Bridge on the River Kwai

(1957) As he would do with *Lawrence of Arabia*, director David Lean builds a big, stirring war epic—and then asks all sorts of annoying questions. Is the stiff-lipped British colonel/Japanese POW (Alec Guinness) a hero for standing up for his men's rights or a fool for building a bridge that will benefit only his captors? Is the American soldier (William Holden) on a mission to destroy that bridge an opportunist or a different kind of hero? Amid the pounding action—and that damned whistling theme tune—Lean deconstructs the black-and-white morality of war films and comes up with troubling shades of gray.

Oscar Index · Eight nominations; seven wins (including Best Picture and Best Director)

How'd He Do That? · Pierre Boule, who it is said could neither read nor write English, won an Oscar for adapting the screenplay from his novel.

Here's How · A day after the ceremony, Carl Foreman (who, because he was blacklisted, was ineligible to receive an Academy Award) announced that he had written the screenplay.

Building Bridges · In 1985, Foreman and cowriter Michael Wilson were given posthumous Oscars.

45

The Seventh Seal *(1957)* The movie that vaulted Ingmar Bergman to the ranks of the world's great directors was, in fact, the 17th feature he helmed. Perhaps that's why it feels confident in purpose and serenely sure in the telling. A medieval allegory that asks modern questions about God, man, and faith, *Seal* lacks the harrowing ambiguities of such later Bergman classics as *Persona* and *Shame*. Instead, as knight Max von Sydow returns from the Crusades to a Europe racked by plague and stalked by Death, the film takes doubt and optimism and plays them off each other like beautifully wrought chess pieces.

Oscar Index · No nominations

Where They Got the Idea · Bergman was inspired, in part, by haunting childhood recollections of medieval paintings and carvings from churches where his minister father preached.

Oops! · Lights from buildings next to the studio are visible through trees at the witch's execution.

Death Takes a Holiday · The famous "dance of death" scene was not performed by the cast. Several actors had left after the movie wrapped for the day, and the sequence was shot using technicians, assistants, and two bewildered set visitors—all in silhouette.

King Kong *(1933)* The story goes that codirector Merian C. Cooper promised actress Fay Wray the "tallest, darkest leading man in Hollywood." A Tinkertoy fairy tale that continues to awe and delight audiences, *Kong* set rules for special-effects extravaganzas we still live by (the hint of something massive over the horizon; the revealing of that something's unthinkable entirety). And yet Kong himself is a lovable schlepp, even when dropping a poor gal whose only crime is that she *isn't* Fay Wray to her death. Mixing horror and the startlingly humane, *Kong* roars still.

Oscar Index · No nominations

Where They Got the Idea · The exploits of explorer and naturalist W. Douglas Burden partly inspired Cooper to make *Kong*.

Sound Advice · Technicians combined lion and tiger sounds, played backward and slowed down, to create Kong's roar.

Censor Sensibility · For a 1938 rerelease, RKO was forced to cut some of Kong's more violent actions (like stomping on a villager and chomping on a shrieking New Yorker) as well as his undressing and fondling of Wray.

Odd Fan · *King Kong* was reportedly a favorite film of Adolf Hitler, who raved about the monster picture for days after seeing it. Hitler is also said to have been very fond of *Snow White and the Seven Dwarfs*.

47

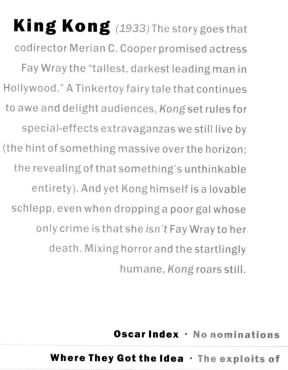

Die Fabel von

KING KONG

Radio
PICTURES

Bonnie and Clyde (1967) Want to blame somebody for the notion of Violence as Trendy Film Accessory? Might as well point at *Bonnie*'s producer-star, Warren Beatty—everyone else did in 1967. But while the old guard clucked and fumed over the slo-mo blood that spattered Arthur Penn's vision of a dust-bowl crime couple, younger audiences were seeing the movie again and again. By turns playful and tragic, knowing and irresponsible, ahistorical and deeply rooted in its period, *Bonnie and Clyde* turned bad guys into counterculture heroes—without letting them *or* the audience off the hook.

Oscar Index · Ten nominations; two wins
(Best Supporting Actress and Cinematography)

Eeeewwww! · When producer Beatty decided to
star, he nixed his sister, Shirley MacLaine,
whom he would have had to kiss on the mouth.

What Did They Know? · Capping a long career
of sometimes out-of-touch reviews, *New York
Times* film critic Bosley Crowther panned the film
and soon left the paper of record.

Catholic Tastes · The National Catholic
Office for Motion Pictures named the film 1967's
"best film for mature audiences."

48

Oscar Index · No nominations

Roman à Clef Notes · Curtis' press agent was reportedly modeled on big-shot Gotham publicist Irving Hoffman; Lancaster's columnist, on big-shot gossipmonger Walter Winchell.

Location, Location, Location · The movie was filmed at many Manhattan hot spots, such as the 21 Club, the Brill Building, and Toots Shor's.

Dislocation · But it was the Active Exterminating Company that was transformed into Joe Robard's club.

True Tales · Co-screenwriter Clifford Odets was decrying the smear tactics employed by many powerful members of the media in the subplot about a musician who is branded a Communist.

49

Sweet Smell of Success

(1957) One of the cinema's great sleepers, it's the kind of film that blows you away when you stumble across it on cable at 3 a.m. Tony Curtis, in the role of his life, plays Sidney Falco, a New York PR flack whose chutzpah almost fills the hole where his morals should be; Burt Lancaster is J.J. Hunsecker, a malevolently powerful gossip columnist with an unhealthy interest in his own sister. The latter rules the rainy nighttime streets off Broadway; the former scurries around the edges, looking for any way in. Like a Weegee photo unstuck in time, *Smell* captures Manhattan's glitz and sleaze—and shows them to be inextricably linked.

Double Indemnity *(1944)* "How could I have known that murder can...smell like honeysuckle?" muses
Walter Neff (Fred MacMurray), the ultimate sap in *the* classic Venus-flytrap noir. *Indemnity* inspired everything from *Body
Heat* to a zillion direct-to-video "erotic thrillers," but the acrid, chintzy doom of Billy Wilder's original is unmatched. Scripted
by Wilder and Raymond Chandler, the film is a mocking vision of middle-class greed, lust, and stupidity, with bored
housewife Phyllis Dietrichson (Barbara Stanwyck) a peroxided cynosure of evil leading the insurance man down to hell.

Oscar Index · Seven nominations; no wins

There's No Justice · Edward G. Robinson (above), so marvelous as claims investigator Barton Keyes, never received an Oscar nomination in his 50-year career.

Original Casting · Alan Ladd, James Cagney, Spencer Tracy, Gregory Peck, and the ubiquitous George Raft all turned down the role that went to Fred MacMurray.

Where They Got the Idea · The film is based on James M. Cain's story of the same name, which was inspired in part by the real-life case of Ruth Snyder and Judd Gray, who were executed for their crime.

Fine-tuning the Concept · Wilder wanted to end his film with Walter's execution in the San Quentin gas chamber (above). But after second thoughts, he finished the movie with Walter confessing into a dictation machine as he bleeds slowly to death from a bullet fired by Phyllis.

5O

Oscar Index · One nomination; no wins

Lost in Translation · In French, the title *Les Enfants du Paradis* is a colloquialism that refers to the common people who sit in a theater's upper balcony.

An Affair to Forget · The film's most prominent wartime casualty was star Arletty, who was imprisoned soon after filming—and the war—had ended, for having had an affair with a German officer.

Oscar Index · Four nominations; three wins (Original Score, Film Editing, and Sound)

Fine-tuning the Concept · In Peter Benchley's novel, the shark kills Hooper (Dreyfuss) and gets away.

Polishing the Script · *Jaws'* signature monologue, about the sinking of the USS *Indianapolis*, was written in 15 minutes by an uncredited John Milius.

Children of Paradise

(1945) It may be the *French*est of French films; certainly it's one of the most beloved. This intensely romantic celebration of social outcasts was shot under the noses of Nazi occupation forces, with hunted Resistance members squirreled away in the crew. The film transcends politics, though: Set in 1840s Paris, it tells of the men and melodrama circling the stage actress Garance, played by Arletty with an ineffable, sphinxlike sexiness. As tightly constructed (*and* enjoyable) as a soap opera, *Paradise* flows with beauty, sadness, and the quietly assured wisdom of a people under siege.

52

Jaws *(1975)* There are people who disdain it as the blockbuster that kicked off the Age of Blockbusters, the film that spoiled the funky '70s party. But—come on—how can you hate something so thrillingly made, so sure in its narrative, so nerve-shreddingly entertaining? From the first subaquatic stirrings of John Williams' brilliant score to the final shot of Roy Scheider and Richard Dreyfuss dog-paddling back from their rendezvous with the leviathan, *Jaws* reclaims craft, character, and pacing and reminds us why these are moviemaking virtues. It's a pop masterpiece—and it established Steven Spielberg as the true heir to the greats of the studio system.

Invasion of the Body Snatchers

Invasion of the Body Snatchers *(1956)* The first movie to explicitly connect modern alienation with—*duh*—aliens, *Invasion* has been interpreted as both an anticommunist and an *anti*-anticommunist parable. In fact, it's simply about the individual's terror of being swallowed by the conformist mob. That notion is so increasingly relevant that the film's been remade twice (both times well) and serves as the model for such developments as *The X-Files*. But Don Siegel's original has the edge for sheer middle-American creepiness, as Kevin McCarthy scampers through Santa Mira just ahead of the Pod People, desperately fending off sleep. Don't forget: *You're next.*

WALTER WANGER CREATES THE ULTIMATE IN SCIENCE-FICTION!

ALLIED ARTISTS presents

INVASION OF THE BODY SNATCHERS

FILMED IN **SUPERSCOPE**

starring KEVIN McCARTHY · DANA WYNTER

with LARRY GATES · KING DONOVAN · CAROLYN JONES · JEAN WILLES · RALPH DUMKE · Directed by DON SIEGEL · Screenplay by DANIEL MAINWARING · Based on the COLLIER'S MAGAZINE Serial by JACK FINNEY

Oscar Index · No nominations

Where They Got the Idea · *Invasion* is based on Jack Finney's *The Body Snatchers*, which was serialized in *Collier*'s magazine beginning in 1954.

Fine-tuning the Concept · Siegel and screenwriter Daniel Mainwaring gave Finney's more optimistic tale a bleak ending, emphasizing *Invasion*'s implied criticism of McCarthyism.

Cameos · *Invasion*'s script doctor (and future gore auteur) Sam Peckinpah had a bit part as a gas meter reader.

54

53

Oscar Index · No nominations

Racial Remix · Welles tried to provoke racists by making the hero (Charlton Heston) Mexican and his wife (Janet Leigh) a blond goddess.

Clever Casting · Leigh performed despite a broken arm (set in a plaster cast) that was artfully concealed before the camera.

Fleshing Out the Character · Already tipping the scales at more than 300 pounds, Welles added padding, special makeup, and a false nose to make his on-screen appearance even more corpulent.

Touch of Evil (1958) Oh, sure, it's a bona fide

classic now, with the restored 1998 cut playing to adoring art-house audiences. But this was the squalid masterpiece that Orson Welles directed during his years in the wilderness—a sleazy, humane, eye-popping B flick that was recut by Universal Pictures, shipped out on the bottom half of a double bill, and treasured only by buffs for decades. Proof that the director never lost his talent—only the opportunity to showcase it—*Touch* is a film of gaudy excesses, from the show-offy, three-minute opening shot to the unfathomable moral bloat of Welles himself as corrupt police chief Hank Quinlan.

The Graduate *(1967)* "Plastics." "Where have you gone, Joe DiMaggio?" *"Elaine!!"* On these catchphrases, an entire generation hung their romantic disenchantment. And yet Mike Nichols' second film is remarkably clear-eyed about its antihero, a barely formed college grad (Dustin Hoffman, almost 30 at the time) who falls into an adulterous fling with his parents' friend (Anne Bancroft), tails her daughter (Katharine Ross) like a lovestruck stalker, and is still floundering in the deep end of the pool at film's end. Youth audiences claimed Benjamin as one of their own, but surely the film's greatness lies in the remorseless uncertainty of its final shot. PHOTOGRAPHS BY BOB WILLOUGHBY

Oscar Index · Seven nominations; one win (Best Director)

Original Casting · Future talk-show host Charles Grodin turned down the role of Benjamin Braddock.

It Was More Like *August*-December · "Older woman" Bancroft was Hoffman's senior by only six years.

Bus Exhaustion · The 40-second scene in which Benjamin chases the bus carrying Elaine took many hours to shoot. Holding up the works: a noisy garbage truck, unruly Hell's Angels, and a street full of oblivious shoppers.

Coo-coo-ka-choo, Mrs. Robinson · An ad showing Hoffman and Bancroft in bed was removed from the New York City subway system after it was deemed "objectionable" and "in poor taste."

Cameos · Richard Dreyfuss plays a resident of the Berkeley rooming house, and screenwriter Buck Henry is a desk clerk at the hotel.

Oscar Index · Five nominations; no wins

Humble Hero · *Life* was Stewart's first movie upon returning from WWII. A clause in his contract forbade any publicity use of his distinguished combat record.

The Birth of a Classic · *Life* became a holiday staple in the 1970s, after its copyright was not renewed and the movie lapsed into public domain—meaning broadcasters could air it without having to pay royalties.

56

It's a Wonderful Life

(1946) As homespun as this small-town fantasy plays today, it wasn't always beloved. In fact, back in 1946, *Life* was a qualified fiasco that ended Frank Capra's dreams of independence—a dark work that must have tasted like rancid eggnog to postwar audiences. George Bailey's a guy whose dreams of getting out of his small town are never realized, and Jimmy Stewart slowly intensifies the character's bitterness until it explodes with naked, suicidal despair. All the angels and happy endings in Hollywood can't erase the harsh taste of where this movie goes; it's that unbecoming honesty, rather than Capra's soothing corn, that lodges in our memories.

The Wild Bunch *(1969)* The film that either killed the Western or followed through on all the genre's romanticized violence by placing slaughter front and center. (Take your pick, but see it.) Sam Peckinpah's crowning work is a controversial, visceral, and even quietly moving saga of frontier's end, with an aging criminal gang (led by William Holden) battling bounty hunters and the Army before finding one last, doomed shot at redemption by protecting villagers from Mexican bandits. Seen today (especially in the restored 1994 director's cut), the gore looks comparatively tame—but its vision of 19th-century men swamped by modernity plays more compellingly than ever.

57

Oscar Index · Two nominations; no wins

Gross-Out Vérité · Not content with entry wounds, Peckinpah used squibs (exploding packets of red dye, used to fake gunshot wounds) on *both* sides of actors' bodies to simulate bullets going in one side and coming out the other.

Gulp! · The bullets were real except when there was an actor in front of them. Peckinpah reportedly used more than 90,000 live rounds during filming.

The Rules of the Game

(1939) "People always have good reasons," says one of the characters, and it could have been the motto for Jean Renoir's entire career—a mocking, democratic sigh at the ways of men. Arguably his greatest work (*Grand Illusion* is the other candidate), *Rules* sets loose a gallery of French types during a weekend country retreat, coupling and uncoupling before falling apart in a spasm of random tragedy. Renoir called it "an exact description of the bourgeois of our time," and needless to say, it didn't go over well in prewar Paris. Today, the foolish wisdom of such characters as Marcel Dalio's marquis and the gruff Octave (Renoir himself) looks more wearily up-to-date than ever.

Oscar Index · No nominations

Auguste Lineage · Renoir was a son of Impressionist painter Pierre Auguste Renoir.

First Impressions · A financial and critical failure when released, *Rules* succeeded only in offending the Nazis, who banned it.

Second Impressions · Two decades later, at the 1959 Venice film festival, the movie was rediscovered and at last recognized as a masterwork.

If at First You Don't Succeed... · After its poor initial reception, Renoir repeatedly reedited *Rules*, cutting most of his own scenes as the rotund Octave. (In the restored version, viewers can enjoy the spectacle of Renoir trapped in a ridiculous bear costume.)

59

The Lady Eve *(1941)* How to pick from the incomparably demented films of Preston Sturges? The man was sui generis in golden-era Hollywood: a writer-director—household name so literate that his ribaldry sailed over the heads of censors, so gut funny that he was beloved of critics and audiences alike. *Sullivan's Travels* may be Sturges' best-known film, but *Eve* is probably his least cluttered and most flat-out hilarious. In this dandy piece of high-handed screwball, a doofus beer heir (Henry Fonda, gloriously dim) gets fleeced twice—first for money, then for love—by con gal Barbara Stanwyck, who sizes up her prey and comments, "I need him like the ax needs the turkey."

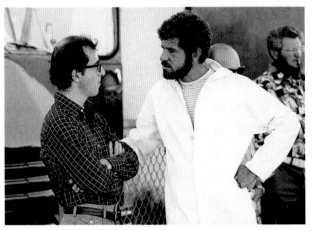

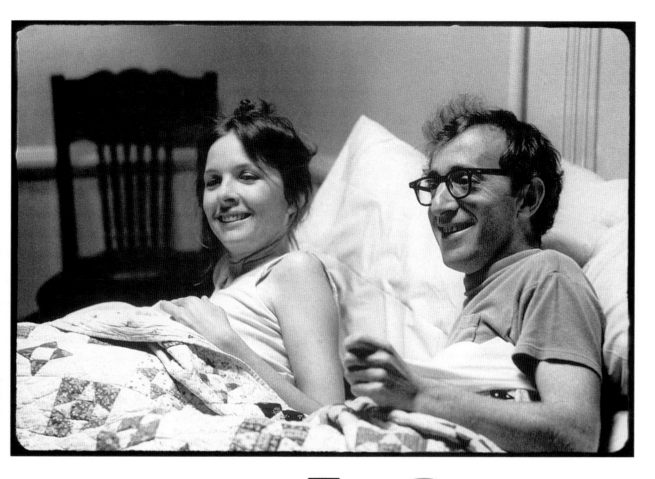

Annie Hall

(1977) Perched on the fence post dividing Funny Woody from Serious Woody, *Annie Hall* is the rare film to showcase a comic genius blossoming into profundity. It's a time-capsule delight, of course, with Diane Keaton's floppy couture rivaling Allen's cocaine sneeze for sheer 1977 zeitgeist. But the gentle way the Woodman peels back the layers of relationships (his real one with Keaton, the fake one on the screen, the ones we ourselves live with) is timeless. As Allen says when he pulls media theorist Marshall McLuhan into the frame to silence a movie-line gasbag, "Boy, if life were only like this!"

PHOTOGRAPHS BY BRIAN HAMILL

101

The Adventures of Robin Hood

(1938) By all accounts, Errol Flynn was a boozing, womanizing wastrel in real life. This only goes to prove, perhaps, why we need movies. In *Robin Hood*—the costume adventure that set the bar for all that followed—Flynn is unbearably lithe, impossibly dashing, irresistibly righteous. The marvel is that the movie keeps up with him all the way, from Erich Wolfgang Korngold's landmark score to Basil Rathbone's sneering Sir Guy to the marvelous motley of Warner's stock-company Merry Men. Add a thoroughbred pace and glowing Technicolor sets, and you have the Hollywood equivalent of an illuminated manuscript—crossed with a really good comic book.

61

Oscar Index · Four nominations; three wins (Film Editing, Original Score, and Art Direction)

Original Casting · James Cagney walked out in a contract dispute and was replaced by Flynn.

Gulp! · Stuntmen were paid $150 per shot for having professional marksmen shoot arrows into their padded clothing.

Oops! · In the jumping-from-the-gallows-onto-horseback scene, Flynn's wrists are clearly tied behind his back at the beginning and end of the shot—but in midair, his hands are in front of his body.

62

Oscar Index · Four nominations; no wins

Auteur Trepidation · Only after Olivier had failed
to talk William Wyler, Carol Reed, and Terence
Young into directing the film did he reluctantly
agree to make his directorial debut with *Henry V.*

Original Casting · Olivier wanted his then-wife
Vivien Leigh to play princess Catherine, but David
O. Selznick refused to let her out of her contract.

Censor Sensibility · The words *damn* and *bastard*
were excised for the film's 1946 U.S. release.

Cheerio! · Producer Filippo Del Giudice,
who fled Mussolini's Italy (and produced another
fervently patriotic British wartime film, *In Which
We Serve*), was instrumental in funding *Henry V.*
For his trouble, Del Giudice was arrested as an
enemy alien at the end of the war. He later sought
refuge in a monastery.

Henry V *(1944)* Half a century before Shakespeare was the hip source for high school date flicks, producer-director-star Laurence Olivier did right by the Bard, by Britain, and by audiences with this dazzling Technicolor treatment of the playwright's most complexly heroic work. By moving his camera slowly into a 17th-century Globe theater production of *Henry* until it miraculously turns real, Olivier guided viewers toward a stunning reenactment of the Battle of Agincourt—and helped England's morale go once more into the breach during the darkest days of World War II. Bursting with ingenuity and tempered high spirits, *Henry* has the freshness of a brilliant fanfare.

63

Oscar Index · No nominations

Previous Career Highlights · Like many French New Wave
auteurs, Godard was once a film critic.

Pop-Culture Obsessions · Godard dedicated *Breathless* to
Monogram—a low-rent B-movie mill that churned out
numerous Westerns and serials in the 1930s and '40s.

What Did They Know? · TIME magazine called *Breathless* "a
sort of ad-lib epic, a Joycean harangue of
images in which the only real continuity is the
irrational coherence of nightmare."

Breathless *(1960)* A perfect
title for the movie that made movies
seem new again. Jean-Luc Godard's
debut, a raffish account of a French
hood (Jean-Paul Belmondo) and his
American girlfriend (Hollywood
expatriate Jean Seberg), is the film
that, with Truffaut's *The 400 Blows*,
kicked off the French New Wave,
and you can still see the director's
influence in the jump cuts and
unsynchronized sound of today's
strenuously hip TV ads. But it was the
sheer streetwise glamour of Belmondo
and Seberg that made the film a
sensation—and that can still make
you breathless 40 years later.

Mean Streets *(1973)*

Who knew that this messy, noisy
Sicilian slice of New Yawk life would be
the blueprint for a generation of indie
films? Who knew if we'd ever hear
from the director, some gonzo kid
named Scorsese, again? Pitching us
headfirst into the skronk of Little
Italy, *Streets* offers an achingly tender
Harvey Keitel as a tough kid
uncovering his soul, Robert De Niro
snapping like a Method-trained pit bull
as his loose-cannon buddy, and a
soundtrack that, by scoring the action
to the Ronettes and the Rolling Stones,
Eric Clapton and Johnny Ace, turns the
film into the best kind of rock opera.

64

Oscar Index · No nominations

Where They Got the Idea · The title was suggested by critic-
screenwriter Jay Cocks, who quoted Scorsese a line from
Raymond Chandler: "Down these mean streets a man must go."

Fine-tuning the Concept · Roger Corman, who had produced
Scorsese's previous feature *Boxcar Bertha*, offered to finance
Mean Streets if Scorsese would agree to an all-black cast.

Through a Lens, Darkly · That gritty, urban look was a matter of
necessity: It rained most of the six days during which Scorsese
could shoot on location in New York—and he didn't have the
lights to properly illuminate many of the interior scenes.

65

The Third Man (1949)

Orson Welles didn't direct it—he only played the supporting role of Harry Lime and wrote the character's devastating Ferris-wheel monologue—but *The Third Man* bristles with the master's nasty mischief. Joseph Cotten plays writer Holly Martins—a nice guy in America, no doubt, but an out-of-his-depth fool in postwar Vienna—who arrives only to hear that his old friend Harry is dead. But Harry's not dead, though maybe he should be, given what he's been up to. From Graham Greene's script to Robert Krasker's cinematography to Anton Karas' zither score to Carol Reed's taut direction, *Man* is one bewitchingly cynical, sneakily thoughtful thriller.

Oscar Index · Three nominations; one win (Black-and-White Cinematography)

Why He Did It · Welles took the role of Harry Lime to help finance his adaptation of *Othello*.

Gross Stupidity · Rather than take a 20 percent cut of the film, a cash-starved Welles took a $100,000 check. The film was one of the biggest hits Welles ever worked on.

Credit Cad · To get Cotten, exec producer Alexander Korda gave David O. Selznick American distribution rights. In the U.S., the credits read "David O. Selznick presents...A David O. Selznick Production...Produced by David O. Selznick."

Notorious *(1946)* The glossiest of Alfred Hitchcock's early Hollywood films is also his most rhapsodic, with Ingrid Bergman gorgeously confused as a spy in the house of love and Cary Grant her cruel, smitten government superior. Marrying suspected-Nazi Claude Rains to smoke out his secrets, Bergman ends up playing emotional S&M with her boss while Hitch's camera ecstatically careens off the walls; in one celebrated scene, he swoops from a wide shot of a party all the way in to a crucial key held in Bergman's hand. And then there's that censor-busting three-minute make-out session—so sensual that the rest of the film feels primed to explode.

Oscar Index · Two nominations; no wins

Original Casting · Hitchcock initially wanted Clifton Webb for the role that went to Rains.

Elevated Performance · The vertically challenged Rains played many of his scenes opposite the much taller Bergman while standing on a box.

Censor Sensibility · For the erotically charged sequence in which Grant and Bergman kiss passionately, Hitchcock artfully dodged the censor's "three-second" rule by having the actors alternate kisses with sensual embraces and smoldering stares.

66

67

Oscar Index · No nominations

Cheap Jokes · *Airplane!* was made for a little more than
$3 million and raked in more than $80 million.

Where They Got the Idea · *Airplane!* most directly parodies
1957's *Zero Hour*, which contained such classic, not-meant-
to-be-funny lines as, "We have to find somebody who can not
only fly this plane, but who didn't have fish for dinner."

Graham Cracker · Nielsen had studied dance with Martha
Graham before his film debut in the mid-1950s.

112

Oscar Index · One nomination ; no wins

Original Casting · Louise Brooks was considered for the bride; Claude Rains for Dr. Pretorius.

Speaking Frankensteinly · The monster's baby-talk vocabulary was culled from the test papers of Universal's child actors.

Method Acting · Lanchester modeled the she-monster's robotic movements on those of German actress Brigitte Helm in Fritz Lang's silent classic, *Metropolis*.

Look Like an Egyptian · Lanchester's monster tresses were inspired by portraits of Queen Nefertiti.

The Bride of Frankenstein

(1935) In the 1998 art-house hit *Gods and Monsters*, *The Bride of Frankenstein* plays on a bar TV to viewers utterly bollixed by its playful tone. "Scary is scary, funny is funny—you don't mix them," gripes the barmaid, missing the point of James Whale's irreverent, spooky, and superior follow-up to his 1931 *Frankenstein*. Boris Karloff immeasurably deepens the monster's humanity with a mere 44-word vocabulary, mildewy Ernest Thesiger has a high old time as the evil Dr. Pretorius, and the sets glow with feverish imagination. Still, it's Elsa Lanchester you'll remember as the birdlike, alien bride—and as Mary Shelley herself.

Airplane! *(1980)* Surely we jest? No—and *please* stop calling us Shirley. The anarchic writer-director combine of Jerry Zucker, Jim Abrahams, and David Zucker retooled film farce for the media age with this nonstop barrage of riffs (the dumber the better) on the airplane-disaster genre. A raft of beloved Hollywood actors torpedo their images— Leslie Nielsen launched a second career in comedy, but our favorite is Barbara Billingsley (The Beav's mom) speaking jive—and the result is the cinematic equivalent of a prime early *MAD* magazine with a gag in every corner of every shot.

The Conformist (1970)

Only Bernardo Bertolucci could ascribe fascism to repressed homosexuality—and craft a devastating movie in the bargain. Jean-Louis Trintignant plays a chilly intellectual in Mussolini's Italy who wants nothing more than to *belong*—and so is willing to assassinate a former professor. Stefania Sandrelli and Dominique Sanda are outrageously erotic as the women in his life, but Bertolucci and cinematographer Vittorio Storaro steal the show with some of the most painterly visions ever put on film—and a showdown in a sun-dappled woods that will haunt you forever.

Oscar Index · One nomination; no wins

Where They Got the Idea · The film was based on Alberto Moravia's novel of the same name.

Roman à Clef Notes · Bertolucci reportedly gave the professor Jean-Luc Godard's address and telephone number.

Previous Career Highlights · Bertolucci was also a poet who won Italy's coveted Premio Viareggio literary prize at 21.

What Did They Know? · TIME magazine on *The Conformist*: "It is a pity that the scenario cannot quite meet the demands of the mise-en-scène."

70

Beauty and the Beast

(1991) The high-water mark in the Second Coming of Disney. Soaring on a simple belief in the power of love to transform, the movie is blessed with a smart-but-not-smug heroine (voiced by Paige O'Hara), a moving Beast (Robby Benson, of all people), a vain hunk of a bad guy (Richard White), hilarious sidekicks (especially given that they're household appliances), and songs by Alan Menken and the late Howard Ashman that are gloriously witty and surpassingly soulful. It's a reminder that we go to the movies for the same reason we read fairy tales:
to be enchanted.

Oscar Index · Six nominations; two wins (Original Score and Original Song)

For the Record Books · *Beauty* made Oscar history as the first feature-length 'toon to be nominated for Best Picture. It was also the first movie to get three Best Song nominations.

Role Models · Animator Glen Keane had Jackie Gleason in mind when illustrating the Beast: "a guy who's frustrated with himself and trying to control his temper."

A Beast of a Job · The 84-minute film took more than three years (and the work of nearly 600 Disney-ites) to complete.

To Be or Not to Be

(1942) "So they call me 'Concentration Camp Ehrhardt'…" That's an unlikely laugh getter, but, as voiced by hambone Polish actor Jack Benny while he's impersonating a Nazi officer, it's also paralyzingly funny. Such are the fetching contradictions of Ernst Lubitsch's wartime comedy, a film that gives Benny the role of his career, makes fun of Hitler's Germany using conventions swiped from French stage farce, and lets Carole Lombard shine one last, unbelievably sexy time. The actress died in a plane crash shortly thereafter; the film, as daring and sparkling as she, is the best kind of memorial.

Oscar Index · One nomination; no wins

Original Title · United Artists thought *To Be* was too highbrow, until Lubitsch suggested *The Censor Forbids*.

Making Concessions to Good Taste · When Lombard was killed in a plane crash just weeks after the film wrapped, *To Be* was reedited to delete the line "What can happen in a plane?"—adding $35,000 to the budget.

Art Imitates Life · On the day Lubitsch shot a scene in which storm troopers marched down a street, a woman who had just come to America from occupied Poland fainted on the spot.

71

FRITZ LANGS
UDØDELIGE
MESTERVÆRK

THE KIDNAPPER
MED
Peter Lorre

72

Oscar Index · No nominations

First Impressions · Lang recalled that "the Nazis feared the 'murderers' would be thinly veiled persons the audiences would recognize as Nazis. When they found I was concerning myself with mere child murderers, they said, 'Oh, go right ahead, Herr Lang, go right ahead.' The pigs."

Irreconcilable Differences · The screenplay was penned by Lang's wife, who later divorced him and joined the Nazi party.

Whistle While You Work · Lorre whistled a tune from Grieg's *Peer Gynt* suites throughout the film, but unhappy with Lorre's rendition, Lang redid it himself.

M *(1931)* Long before the likes of Hannibal the Cannibal stalked our nightmares, Fritz Lang created this brilliant study of a psychopathic killer, based on the real-life crimes of one Peter Kürten, a.k.a. the "Vampire of Düsseldorf." As the bodies of little girls pile up, and the police grow more frantic, the city's criminal underworld decide to ferret out the murderer—if only so they can get back to work. Their quarry is plump, mild-mannered Hans Beckert, who, in Peter Lorre's astounding performance, finally gains our pity when he shrieks, "I can't help myself!" before the gangland kangaroo court.

Great Expectations *(1946)* The twisty, character-rich works of Charles Dickens have always been natural fodder for movies, but few adaptations have moved with the eerily powerful narrative force of the books. David Lean's *Great Expectations* is the grand exception (with his 1948 *Oliver Twist* running a close second). The tale of an orphan whose mysterious benefactor raises him out of rural poverty into upper-class London is beautifully realized, with stunning photography from Guy Green, note-perfect performances by the entire cast (including John Mills, Alec Guinness, and a young Jean Simmons), and an understanding of social caste and moral character that, for once, bites like the Dickens.

Oscar Index · Five nominations; two wins
(Cinematography and Art Direction)

Oops! · No one noticed when a crew member drew a cartoon
about wartime rationing on the set. It can be seen just above
Pip Pirrip's (John Mills) shoulder when he reunites with Estella.

Censor Sensibility · Hackles were raised over scenes of a
husband and wife in bed; plus, censors feared that Pip's
luxurious digs would tempt "thousands of young boys with no
education to come to London and lead a good life."

Overrated? · Lean talked the censors out of the cuts, but the
film was nonetheless given an "A" certificate (meaning
children could not be admitted without an adult).

73

Funny Face *(1957)* In theory, a 57-year-old Fred Astaire has no business winning a 27-year-old Audrey Hepburn. But these two particular performers never seemed all that real in the first place: They're both phantoms of the screen, elegant tricks of the light. Likewise, Stanley Donen's musical is lovely, ephemeral cotton candy, a melding of Gershwin (songs) and Givenchy (fashion) into witty gossamer. Astaire's a fashion photographer and Hepburn's the Greenwich Village beatnik whose face, he thinks, is the next big thing. It sure is when she falls for him : Hepburn in love practically radiates bliss. And the movie? 'S wonderful.

Oscar Index · Four nominations; no wins

Roman à Clef Notes · Astaire's fashion photographer is based on Richard Avedon, who's credited as visual consultant. Kay Thompson's magazine editor is based on *Harper's Bazaar* honcho Diana Vreeland.

Birth of a Buzzword · Vreeland was famous for looking at layouts and saying they had no *bizzazz*. That word was used in the film and years later (owing to a spelling error) became *pizzazz*.

Signal Achievement · Paramount didn't want Richard Avedon giving Donen any more advice on the set, so he was reduced to using his necktie to communicate. Loosening the knot, for example, meant Donen should widen the aperture of the light.

74

Tootsie *(1982)* As Dustin Hoffman says to Jessica Lange toward the end, "I was a better man with you as a woman than I ever was with a woman as a man." Trust us, it makes sense in the context of this surprisingly touching cross-dressing farce. Everything clicks, from the deft script by Larry Gelbart and Murray Schisgal (with uncredited help from Barry Levinson and Elaine May) to the vision of a soap opera set as a neurotic home away from home to performances of across-the-board grace and hilarity. And Hoffman is sublime as the pesky, out-of-work actor who becomes one hell of a dame.

Oscar Index · Two nominations; no wins

Behind the Scenes · To get a startled-looking flinch from Harvey, director John Frankenheimer fired a toy cannon on the set.

Location, Location, Location · Jilly's bar was used to oblige Sinatra pal Jilly Rizzo.

The Game of the Name · Some members of the army platoon were named after the cast of *The Phil Silvers Show*.

Life Imitates Art · Frankenheimer was supposed to sit next to Robert F. Kennedy at a victory dinner in L.A. on the night he was assassinated.

What Did They Know? · *Films in Review* said, "*The Manchurian Candidate* will seem so incomprehensible you will wonder why it was made...."

75

76

Oscar Index · Ten nominations; one win (Best Supporting Actress)

Titular Trivia · The title came from Hoffman, whose mother "used to throw me up in the air and say, 'How's my tootsie wootsie?'"

Busty Dusty · Hoffman's four-pound silicone breasts (customized by a maker of post-mastectomy prostheses) cost $175 each.

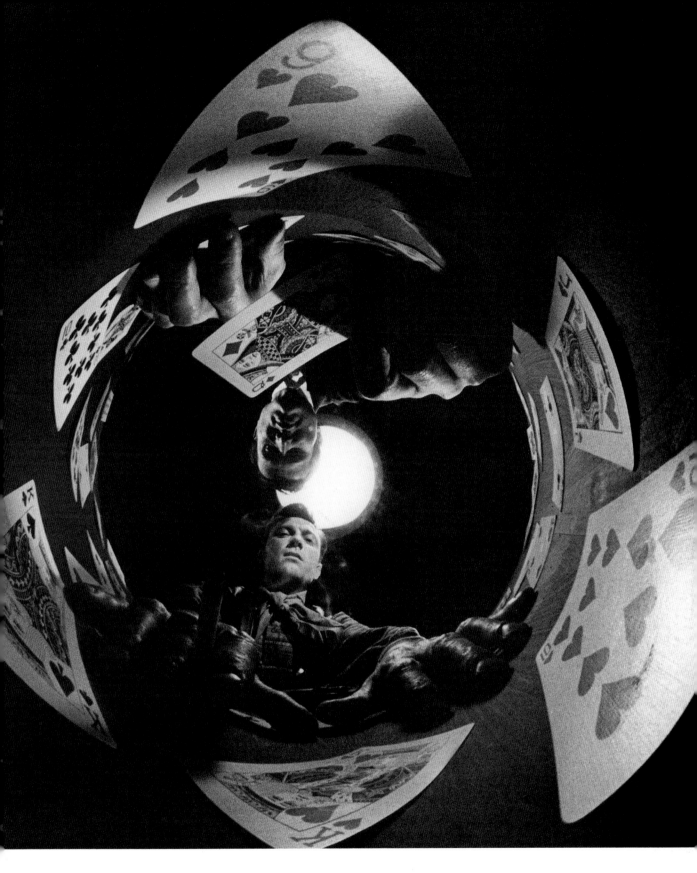

The Manchurian Candidate *(1962)* The most demented political thriller ever made is exciting, funny—and so paranoid that it had to be on to something. As the tenuous voice of sanity, Frank Sinatra pieces together a bizarre assassination plot, woos Janet Leigh in an extremely strange pickup scene, and leads poor, nasty, brainwashed Laurence Harvey to his inevitable reckoning. Featuring Angela Lansbury as the Dragon Lady of movie mothers, *Candidate* was reportedly a favorite of John F. Kennedy's—and rarely surfaced after his death made it seem glib *and* prophetic. Seen today, it foreshadows with glittering lunacy our modern distrust of government, the media, even reality itself.

77

Potemkin *(1925)* Hugely influential, Sergei Eisenstein's silent classic brought film editing to early maturity, and the shock waves it set off still reverberate in music videos, in TV ads—in the very grammar of the filmed entertainment we inhale each day. All of which would depress the director to no end, since this dramatization of a 1905 mutiny on a Russian battleship was the premier artistic offering of the young Communist regime and a paean to the power of the masses. Long after the Lenin statues have been toppled, though, *Potemkin* still enthralls—and the harrowing Odessa steps sequence will be timely as long as governments send their soldiers to fire on civilians.

Oscar Index · Predated the Academy Awards

How They Did It · The steps sequence was filmed partly with a camera strapped to the waist of an acrobat who tumbled down the steps.

Type Casting · Eisenstein cast parts by what he called "typage": searching for faces that matched his idea of each character. The doctor was played by a hotel boiler man; the priest was a gardener.

Down to the Wire · The film was still being edited on the day of its Bolshoi Theatre premiere. As reels were completed, they were rushed to the theatre on a motorcycle and the last reel was held together with spit.

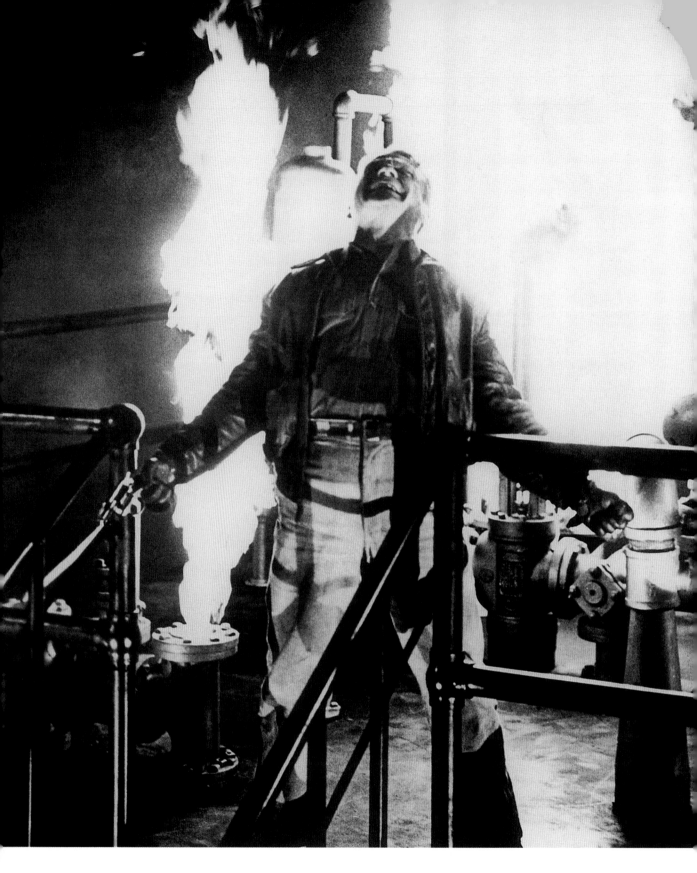

White Heat *(1949)* James Cagney was supposed to have outgrown gangster roles by this time, but the part of Cody Jarrett was just too meaty to turn down: a great screen psycho who flies to pieces before our very eyes. Modeled after one of Ma Barker's sons, Cody's a trigger-happy, textbook case right out of Freud: The scene where he sits in the lap of his beady-eyed old mother (Margaret Wycherly) was Cagney's own inspiration and barely made it past the censors. Raoul Walsh directs without a trace of sentiment, and Cagney never lets up, goosing the character's demons until Cody makes it to the top of the world—and finally, literally explodes.

WHITE HEAT

CHERRILL
MARIS
ALBRIGHT
NEWELL

TED BY
WEBER

Oscar Index · No nominations

Credit Report · Charles Bogle, credited with the original story, is actually Fields' pseudonym.

Previous Career Highlights · Kathleen Howard, who played the nagging Mrs. Bissonette, had previously been an opera singer and fashion editor at *Harper's Bazaar*.

He Didn't Kid Around · Fields disliked children and believed costar Baby LeRoy was out to ruin him. Between takes, the actor would sit in a corner growling threats, and is rumored to have spiked the child's orange juice with gin.

79

78

Oscar Index · One nomination; no wins

Never Satisfied · Despite rave reviews, Cagney called his performance "just another cheapjack job" and longed to return to more wholesome family entertainment.

A Barbaric Yawp · Cody's howl at the news of his mother's death was inspired by the noises Cagney's father made during alcoholic rages.

What the Hell Was That? · The extras in the scene weren't told what was coming, and according to one, the cry "scared the bejesus out of us."

It's a Gift *(1934)* W.C. Fields was unique in pop culture: He despised amusingly. In his most unfettered yet consistently hilarious comedy, he presents the domesticated American male as a kind of petty Job, suffering the indignities of marriage, children, work, and salesmen showing up at five in the morning looking for Carl LaFong. As always, Fields' command of dialogue is a surreal and mighty thing: To a line as simple as "I hate clams," he can impart a spin that will put you in stitches. This is muttering as art—the ultimate protest of a prostrate man.

Nosferatu *(1922)* The creepiest of all vampire films—the one that can paralyze a viewer with dread—is, remarkably, also one of the earliest. F.W. Murnau's silent adaptation of Bram Stoker's *Dracula* doesn't gussy up its bloodsucking antihero in a tux and hair pomade, à la Bela Lugosi. Instead, Count Orlok (Max Schreck) is a bald, ratlike, cadaverous monster—and still he exerts an unnerving erotic pull. Unfolding with the inarguability of a dream, *Nosferatu* presents Death as the ultimate lover with high style and no illusions: In a very real way, it's the missing link between 19th-century gothic and late-20th-century Goth.

Oscar Index · Predated the Academy Awards

The Game of the Name · Max Schreck's last name means "terror" in German.

Art Director Imitates Life · The mysterious lease that Hutter brings to Count Orlok comes from art director Albin Grau's fascination with the occult. A devoted spiritualist, Grau filled the letter with cabalistic and astrological symbols.

She Should've Tried a Wooden Stake · Florence Stoker (widow of *Dracula* author Bram Stoker) sued Prana-Film for copyright infringement and won an order that all prints and negatives of *Nosferatu* be destroyed.

You Can't Kill the Undead · Pirated copies of the film surfaced in England and America, and one was even screened at a benefit that Florence Stoker was asked to attend (she declined the invitation).

Oscar Index · Two nominations; no wins

Quick Study · Lee penned the script in two weeks.

Original Casting · Lee wrote the part of Sal (which eventually went to Danny Aiello) with Robert De Niro in mind.

Uncle Tommaso · "When I saw that the part was for a guy who owned a pizza parlor, I stopped reading right there," Aiello said of his initial reaction to the script. "That's the Italian version of asking a black guy to play a watermelon farmer."

What Did They Know? · *The Village Voice* accused Lee of "Afro-Fascist chic."

The Director Speaks · "The film was made to provoke thought and discussion. We want to bring the spotlight back onto the issue of racism."

8 1

Do the Right Thing *(1989)* It comes out of the '80s time capsule as one of the few films to plumb
the cracks driven into American society during the Reagan years. Which sounds awfully fusty, except that the thing *teems*
with life, as if writer-director Spike Lee had focused his microscope on one sweltering Brooklyn street corner and
watched as the world walked by. Spinning with human tenderness, racial rage, and the joy of making movies, *Do the Right
Thing* caused mass freak-outs within the (mostly white) media establishment when it was released. A decade later, after
the L.A. riots and allegations of police brutality in New York, it looks prescient, democratic—and right.

131

Glutton for Punishment · The suspense reportedly caused at least one filmgoer to faint. Revived, she insisted on going back to see the shocking conclusion.

Signed in Blood · Patrons at some theaters were asked to sign a statement swearing they wouldn't reveal the ending to their friends.

Diabolique

Diabolique *(1955)* It's as twisty as a Hitchcock thriller—and as nightmarishly squalid as that weed-choked pool where a corpse may or may not lie. Nobody is particularly pleasant in Henri-Georges Clouzot's creepy tale of a timid wife (Vera Clouzot) and a brassy mistress (Simone Signoret) who conspire to bump off the man in their lives (nasty schoolmaster Paul Meurisse). Yet you can't help feeling awful for the women when the body up and disappears—then seems to come back for a little revenge. One of the great psychological horror films, *Diabolique* strands a viewer between distaste and delicious fear.

The Best Years of Our Lives

The Best Years of Our Lives *(1946)* After a half decade of happy-faced WWII propag[anda,] Hollywood balanced the scales with William Wyler's devastating drama about returning vets, one of the most emoti[onally] honest movies to come out of the dream factory. It's tough to pick out the most heartbreaking moment: stolid b[anker] Fredric March realizing that he's as unrecognizable to his children as they are to him; war hero–turned–soda jer[k Dana] Andrews reliving a battle in the nose of an abandoned plane; double amputee Harold Russell letting his fiancée dre[ss] for bed with abashed frankness. Tough and mournful, *Years* is a bittersweet eulogy for American inno[cence.]

Oscar Index · Eight nominations; seven wins (including Best Actor, Best Director, and Best Picture)

Type Casting · Russell, who won Best Supporting Actor, was not a professional actor; he was a veteran who had lost both hands in a hand-grenade explosion.

Behind the Scenes · Director Wyler insisted that the cast wear their own clothes and use little or no makeup.

What Might Have Been · Oscar winner March originally planned on a career in banking.

Blow-Up *(1966)* Two movies, really: One's the ne plus ultra of the Swinging Sixties genre, with amoral London fashion photographer David Hemmings scampering through a whirlwind of bored models, hot-to-trot teens, and tennis-playing mimes. The other begins when Hemmings examines the pictures he has taken in a park—and slowly realizes he has photographed a murder. The first film is a wonderful, goofy nostalgia trip, right down to the Yardbirds smashing a guitar. The second—and far deeper one—expands on that signal truth of our times as first posited by the Zapruder film: The closer we look…the less we know.

Oscar Index · Two nominations; no wins

How They Did It · For one scene, director Michelangelo Antonioni had assistants cover 200 yards of a road with 300 gallons of black paint and paint the front of a nearby house white for contrast.

Catholic Tastes · The National Catholic Office for Motion Pictures said: "Brilliance of camera technique and beauty of image composition do not justify a sexual treatment which…will impress viewers as going beyond reasonable limits of moral acceptability."

85

Oscar Index · Eight nominations; three wins (including Best Actor and Adapted Screenplay)

We Knew Them When · Robert Duvall made his screen debut in the small but pivotal role of Boo Radley.

Location, Location, Location · The frame houses in *To Kill a Mockingbird* were removed from a run-down neighborhood in Los Angeles and rebuilt on a studio lot to resemble a Southern town.

To Kill a Mockingbird (1962) Unfolding with

the spooky clarity of a tomboy's memories, Robert Mulligan's Deep South drama is cherished both for its knowledge of the monsters, real and imagined, that are out there in the back of the yard, and for Gregory Peck's weary omnipotence as Atticus Finch, lawyer and dad. Atticus, in fact, served as ultimate father figure for legions of baby boomers; his handsome charisma and liberal beliefs offered, in a sense, a cinematic mirroring of then President John F. Kennedy's. It's a tribute to *Mockingbird*'s gentle power that Atticus, at least, still stands tall: To watch this movie now is to rewind our idealism to the start.

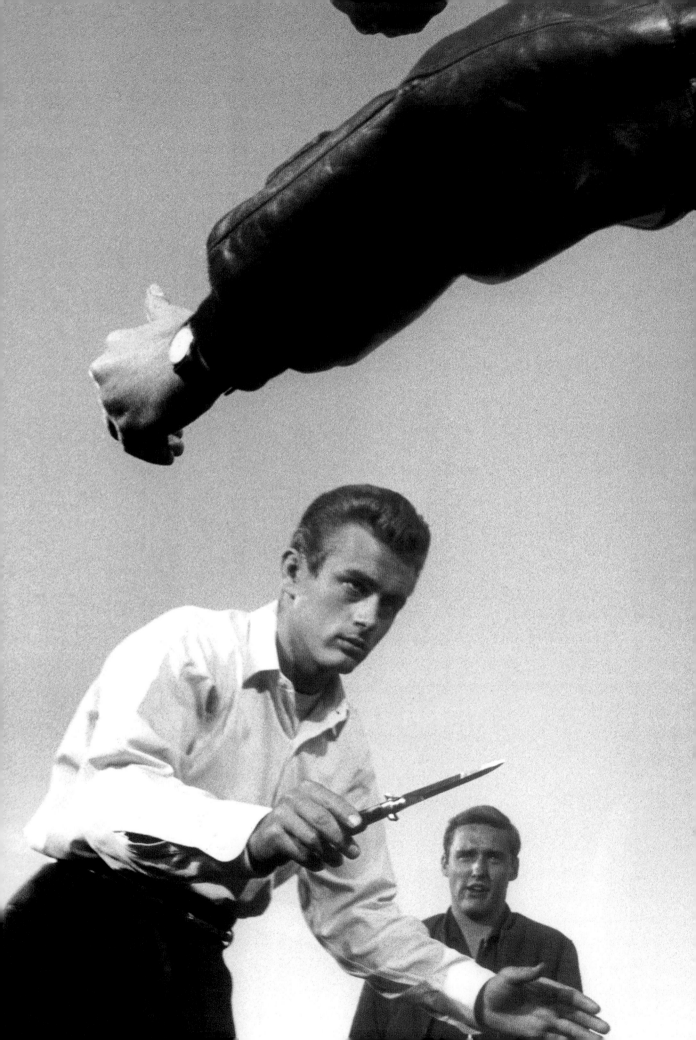

86

Oscar Index · Three nominations; no wins

Was It Wagner or the Wine? · Dean prepped for his emotional police station scene by drinking wine and listening to "Ride of the Valkyrie" in his dressing room while cast and crew were kept waiting. When he finally emerged, he pulled it off in one take.

Location, Location, Location · The character Plato's house and pool were also used in *Sunset Boulevard* (No. 28).

Rebel Without a Cause (1955) The film
that lives up to the James Dean mystique, makes the case for director Nicholas Ray as one of Hollywood's most overlooked poets, and is one of the finest wide-screen movies ever made (to watch it cropped for video is to cheat yourself out of half a movie), *Rebel* is first and foremost the arrival of a true teenage sensibility in pop culture. With Dean, Natalie Wood, and Sal Mineo seeming to pour their souls onto the screen, it's an impressionistic cry of adolescent pain that still echoes in our culture: Everything from *Saturday Night Fever* to *Dawson's Creek* works in its shadow.

L'Age d'Or *(1930)* As ferocious, funny, and liberating as a dream, Luis Buñuel's *L'Age d'Or* brought the Golden Age of French Movie Surrealism to a close: Right-wing critics trashed the Paris theater where it was playing, and the movie was banned in many countries (including the U.S.) for 50 years. You can still see why: With finger-sucking hero Gaston Modot making mad mud-love to Lya Lys, fathers who shoot their sons over minor offenses, bishops being thrown out of windows, and a sadistic libertine who turns out to be Christ, *L'Age* remains a passionate, shockingly fresh appeal for individual freedom.

The Producers *(1968)* The Borscht Belt meets sick humor in this funny, sweet-tempered classic about a type A theatrical producer (Zero Mostel), his grade-A nebbish accountant (Gene Wilder), and a musical called *Springtime for Hitler*. They've sold 25,000 percent of the show, so it had *better* be a flop, but what the poor saps don't know—and what Mel Brooks, making his directorial debut, does—is that the Age of Irony is arriving just in time for the curtain. *Springtime* is a demented delight, of course, but it's Mostel and Wilder—horseradish and honey mustard—who stick to your ribs.

Oscar Index · Two nominations; one win (Original Screenplay)

Previous Career Highlights · Brooks wrote for Sid Caesar in the 1950s and created the TV series *Get Smart* with Buck Henry in 1965.

Art Imitates Art · The director had a stock answer for the questions about what his next project would be—It was writing and directing a movie called *Springtime for Hitler*.

Wings of Desire (1988) The films
of Wim Wenders have always possessed an
otherworldly grace, but this one puts the seraphim on
the screen for all to see, and the result is a vast,
humane epic of the soul. Bruno Ganz and Otto Sander
are the sad-faced angels floating among the people
of Walled-off Berlin, eavesdropping on private sorrows
and imparting invisible shivers of joy. Then Ganz
falls in love and falls to earth.... Funny, sad, and wise,
Wings soars on emotions as rich as its imagery.

89

Pickup on South Street (1953) One of the great forgotten movies of the '50s. Richard Widmark, his
tiny face taut under a snap-brim, plays the pickpocket who snatches top secret microfilm wanted by both the FBI and the
Commies. Writer-director Sam Fuller is less interested in Red-baiting, though, than in watching his outcast characters
come in from the cold. It's peak noir, as dizzying as a bebop sax solo, and Widmark is memorable as a guy who can punch
a woman out, revive her by pouring cold beer on her head, and then passionately neck with her a minute later.

Oscar Index · No nominations

Winging It · Some of Peter Falk's bits were improvised. "I had to come up with a good hat, so that became a scene, and Wim saw me sketching, which I always do to pass the time, and we put that in the movie, too."

The Director Speaks · "I was...tired of a certain notion—that there's no future, that nothing works anymore between men and women.... So I wanted to make a very positive love story."

90

Oscar Index · One nomination; no wins

Location, Location, Location · Though *Pickup* is set in gritty New York, Fuller shot the film in a studio and "not-so-beautiful parts of Los Angeles."

Sense of Direction · Fuller staged Widmark and Richard Kiley's fight on a staircase because: "I wanted to...hear [Kiley's] chin smack each step."

The Fuller Brush-off · Despite the fact that FBI director J. Edgar Hoover was offended by the scene in which a G-man bribes a snitch to get information, it stayed in.

Big-Bang Theory · Because Widmark was not amused by Fuller's habit of firing a pistol to signal the beginning of each scene, the director reluctantly agreed to keep his roscoe packed.

Mildred Pierce *(1945)* Cross film noir with a women's weepie and you get Michael Curtiz's masochistic tale of mother love, murder, and homemade pies. Joan Crawford's shoulder-padded resolve in the face of a failed first marriage, a caddish second husband, and—worst of all—an ungrateful devil daughter (sexy little Ann Blyth) totters on the edge of camp. But there's neurotic greatness in the biting script (based on James M. Cain's novel), swank visuals (by master cinematographer Ernest Haller), and the brittle, unyielding conviction of the star.

91

Oscar Index · Six nominations; one win (Best Actress)

Original Casting · Bette Davis, Ann Sheridan, and Rosalind Russell all turned down the role that earned Crawford an Oscar.

Making a Comeback · Crawford, in need of a comeback after being deemed box office poison, submitted to a screen test and won the role.

Situation Comity · Curtiz had this to say about the possibility of working with Crawford: "She comes over here with her high-hat airs and her goddamn shoulder pads!... Why should I waste my time directing a has-been?"

Piece Offering · While production got off to a bumpy start, the director and star were friends by the end. At the wrap party, Crawford presented Curtiz with a set of Adrian shoulder pads.

Oscar Index · Four nominations; three wins (Best Actress)

Location, Location, Location · The sets were built in forced perspective, with objects in the background smaller than those in the foreground. In city scenes, some skyscrapers were only 25 feet tall, and midgets were used to populate the background.

Method Acting · Murnau had O'Brien put weights in his shoes so that his heavy steps would imply his troubled emotions.

92

Sunrise (1927) For his Hollywood debut, German director F.W. Murnau dared to make a simple romantic fairy tale—shot through with the knowledge of darkness. George O'Brien and Janet Gaynor are the country couple ripped asunder when vamp Margaret Livingston seduces O'Brien in a field (an astonishingly erotic sequence) and convinces him to try to murder his wife. How they find their way back to each other is gorgeously shot and surpassingly benevolent: that Murnau made both this and the blood-freezing *Nosferatu* (No. 80) is the mark of a major—and, sadly, forgotten—artist.

The Road Warrior *(1981)* Sometimes it seems like this is why movies were invented: for the sheer delight of putting bodies in motion. George Miller's second chapter in the Mad Max saga pushes the story into an apocalyptic world of warrior clans, death-mobiles, Feral Kids, and impossible high-speed stunts. In the process Miller invented a new genre, reawakened audiences to the pleasures of kinesis, and delivered unto Hollywood a star (Mel Gibson) on the order of Clark Gable. Yeah, it's a Western in post-punk clothing. It's also the rare film to carve out its own pop frontier.

Oscar Index · No nominations

A Dog's Life · The blue-heeler who plays Max's cleverly named sidekick, Dog, was discovered at a Sydney pound and trained for three months.

Dog-Eared · The pooch had to have his ears plugged to keep him from "completely disgracing himself" during the film's action sequences.

Road Kill · More than half of the 80-plus custom-constructed vehicles were demolished during the production.

The Shop Around the Corner (1940) *You've Got Mail* may have refurbished the plot for the online age, but Ernst Lubitsch's original is unmatched for wise bliss. Jimmy Stewart and Margaret Sullavan play salesclerks who loathe each other at work but exchange passionate anonymous sighs in pen-pal correspondence. *Shop*'s greatness lies in the loneliness and humanity of *all* its characters—especially Frank Morgan as a gruff, wounded boss—and in the way it lets Stewart and Sullavan slowly come down the stepladders of cynicism until, standing toe-to-toe, they recognize each other at last.

Oscar Index · No nominations

Type Casting · Lubitsch cast Stewart because "he holds his public by his very lack of a handsome face or a suave manner."

Not Quite Ready-to-Wear · A stickler for detail even in black and white, Lubitsch thought the $1.98 dress Sullavan bought for Klara to wear looked too smart for a salesclerk and had it faded in the sun and altered to fit poorly.

What's My Line? · Stewart repeatedly flubbed his lines in the final scene, in which Alfred rolls up his pants to prove to Klara he's not bowlegged. Embarrassed by his skinny legs, Stewart redid the scene 48 times—the most in his career.

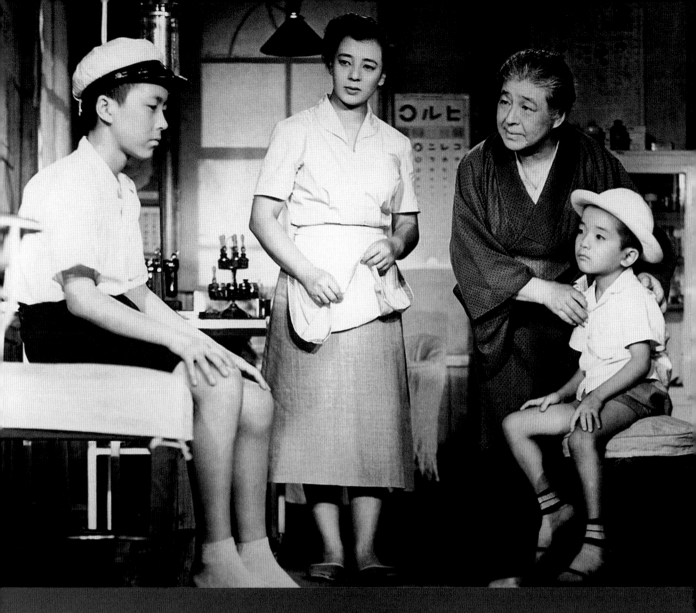

95

Tokyo Story (1953) The most Japanese of Japanese directors, Yasujiro Ozu made films that have the surface calm of a tea ceremony—yet reveal bottomless depths of human joy, sorrow, and yearning. *Tokyo Story* follows an elderly couple who travel to the city to visit their grown children, but into that delicate latticework Ozu packs everything that can be said about the relationship between parent and child: the resentments, the compromises, the need for independence, the ache to connect. If you're looking for a movie to put in the spaceship to explain the human race to aliens, look no further.

Oscar Index · One nomination; one win (Sound)

There's Nothing Like Teamwork · During production, a costume designer walked off the set, a hairstylist quit, a cinematographer was fired, the crew briefly went on strike, and the Native American extras staged a protest over poor working conditions.

Where They Got the Idea · The 1936 version of the film (starring Randolph Scott) was the first movie Mann remembers seeing.

Skills Acquisition · Day-Lewis prepared for the part by spending eight months learning how to run and shoot a musket at the same time.

The Last of the Mohicans

(1992) It's not particularly good history—but, please, neither was the book. And what director Michael Mann wrought from James Fenimore Cooper's classic novel *is* great cinema: Rousing and romantic, it makes the French and Indian War of the 1750s–1760s seem more breathlessly visceral than any modern action flick. It helps, surely, that the leads are glorious to behold: long, lean Daniel Day-Lewis as Cooper's eternal Hawkeye and Madeleine Stowe, flaring her nostrils, as beleaguered Cora Munro. Placing their on-the-run romance at the center of an epic canvas, Mann reminds us that some people *can* make 'em like they used to.

PHOTOGRAPHS BY FRANK CONNOR

97

Oscar Index · Eight nominations; three wins (Best Actress, Best Supporting Actress, Original Screenplay)

Showing His Mickey · *The Piano*, with Keitel's full-frontal nudity, was the first film released by Miramax after it was acquired by Disney.

How They Did It · Cinematographer Stuart Dryburgh employed various techniques to give the film its murky, otherworldly look, inspired by a 19th-century photographic process called Autochrome, in which colors become distorted and intensified.

The Piano

(1993) Of all the hoopskirt dramas that have infested art houses recently, this is the only one that's genuinely, dangerously erotic. Of course it was directed by a woman. Holly Hunter trades in her kudzu eccentricity to play the mute mail-order bride who arrives in 19th-century New Zealand, only to be ineluctably drawn to a half-savage Harvey Keitel while husband Sam Neill beetles his brows and slowly goes crazy. Using potent, eerie imagery—a piano on a vast expanse of beach, a finger gently circling a hole in the heroine's stocking—director Jane Campion creates a sensual thinking woman's romance: Jane Austen Uncorseted.

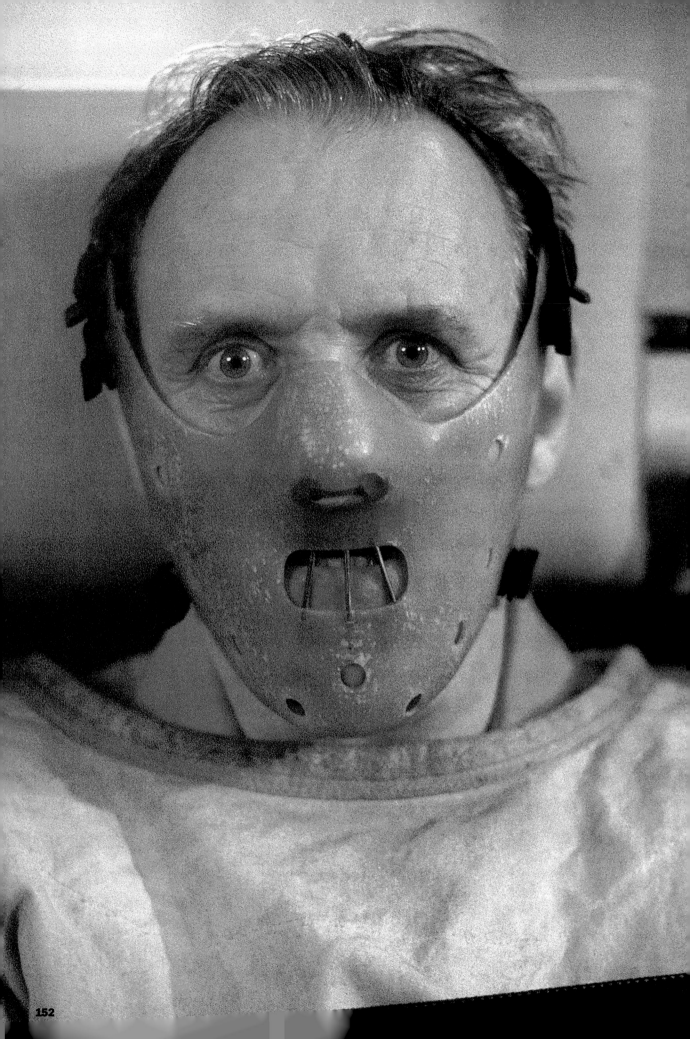

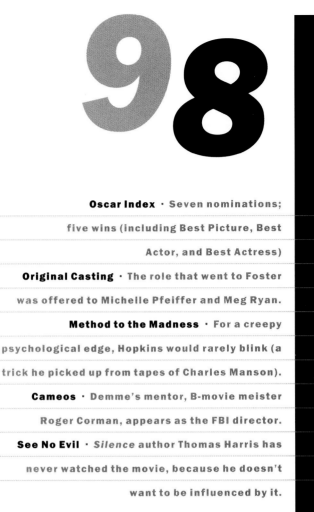

98

The Silence of the Lambs

(1991) A distressing but telling fact of life in the '90s: Hannibal the Cannibal—psychiatrist, gastronome, butcher—is a pop hero. Ascribe that to the American fascination with serial killers, those bogeymen entrepreneurs. Acknowledge the deadpan grimness of Thomas Harris' original novel, Oscar winner Jonathan Demme's spookily precise direction, and the tight-lipped appeal of Jodie Foster as an FBI trainee who seeks the killer's help to catch another monster. But give the real credit to Anthony Hopkins, who makes Hannibal a figure of charm, depth, and irreducible evil. It's a masterful, and nearly satanic, seduction. PHOTOGRAPHS BY KEN REGAN

Oscar Index · Seven nominations; five wins (including Best Picture, Best Actor, and Best Actress)

Original Casting · The role that went to Foster was offered to Michelle Pfeiffer and Meg Ryan.

Method to the Madness · For a creepy psychological edge, Hopkins would rarely blink (a trick he picked up from tapes of Charles Manson).

Cameos · Demme's mentor, B-movie meister Roger Corman, appears as the FBI director.

See No Evil · *Silence* author Thomas Harris has never watched the movie, because he doesn't want to be influenced by it.

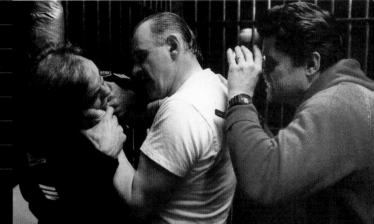

Swept Away *(1975)* Fusing the political and the personal like no director before or since, Italy's Lina Wertmuller made movies that dropped like smart bombs on the complacent early '70s. In this, her most feted, fractious, and controversial comedy, a sleek capitalist rich bitch (Mariangela Melato) and a scraggly Communist deckhand (Giancarlo Giannini) get stranded on a desert island where their roles reverse to the point where she's literally kissing his feet. Years before the term "politically incorrect" was coined, *Swept Away* gleefully staked out the basic terrain, scandalizing feminists, shocking conservatives—pretty much ticking off everybody. Clearly, Wertmuller was doing something right.

Oscar Index · No nominations

A Mouthful · The full title was *Swept Away...by an unusual destiny in the blue sea of August.*

What Did They Know? · American feminist Ellen Willis said that Wertmuller "panders to two classic male-supremacist lies: that women dominate men and that women are parasites while men do all the work."

What Did She Know? · Wertmuller disagreed with her feminist critics, telling TIME magazine "men ought to picket my movies," since she portrayed them as "vain, arrogant... chauvinists who believe in the superiority of the penis."

99

Céline & Julie Go Boating

(1974) Think *Groundhog Day* on a long, lazy French vacation. The most obscure film in this book is also the one that best celebrates the how and why of our love for movies—the ways, in fact, that we use fiction itself to breathe meaning into our lives. It starts slowly, but stick with it: When the two Parisian chums, played by Dominique Labourier and Juliet Berto, stumble into a house where the same melodramatic tale plays out day after day, director Jacques Rivette lifts us into an enchanted storytelling playground, with a climactic title scene that comes as a delicious, goose-pimply release.

100

And No, Forget.

>>> or you're incredibly cheesed at us for choosing,

say, Disney's *Beauty and the Beast* over Cocteau's. Believe us, the folks working on this book had those same arguments (and, hey, we're still friends). One of the annoying anomalies of making these lists is that the movies we often hold dearest sometimes aren't always the "best." Or they may be very, very good—but fall in line somewhere around No. 104 or No. 121. So, in acknowledgment of the fact that, yes, there are more than 100 great movies—and to achieve a semblance of amity in the hallways of ENTERTAINMENT WEEKLY—here are 25 more that somehow didn't make our A list but that are just too beloved to ignore.

<<<
Apocalypse Now *(1979)* Is this the greatest Vietnam movie ever made? Until the woozy final act it is, with Francis Ford Coppola leading his troops into a creepy, chaotic hell on earth. One line sums up the movie *and* the war: "I love the smell of napalm in the morning..."

PHOTOGRAPH BY
MARY ELLEN MARK

e Didn't

By now, you're either dizzy with Great Movie fever »»

The African Queen
(1951) Bogie and Kate Hepburn are up an odd-couple creek without a paddle wheel in John Huston's adorably scruffy romantic adventure. The stars veer perilously close to waterfalls and playful self-parody alike, and the whole thing has the feel of a lark—with leeches.

Five Easy Pieces
(1970) A better movie by far than *Easy Rider*, it embodies the unsettling crosscurrents of the '60s in a piano prodigy–turned–oil rigger who's fleeing both propriety and himself. Jack Nicholson gives the character a crazy charm—and a scary chill.

American Graffiti
(1973) The movie that invented modern nostalgia, hinted at the coming age of blockbusters, and made a Hollywood player out of a shy moviemaker named George Lucas. The cast is vast, the music hops, the tone is wistfully fun.

From Here to Eternity *(1953)* An
engrossing soap opera that plays out under the looming shadow of Pearl Harbor, Fred Zinnemann's adaptation of the James Jones novel lets Montgomery Clift brood beautifully, Burt Lancaster roll in the surf with Deborah Kerr—and Frank Sinatra resurrect his career.

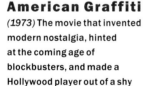

Breakfast at Tiffany's *(1961)*
Hollywood went lightly over adapting Truman Capote's tale of Manhattan courtesan Holly Golightly (Audrey Hepburn), but the result is one of the most knowing romances put on film (once you subtract Mickey Rooney from the equation).

A Hard Day's Night
(1964) Richard Lester's anarchic comedy was made to cash in on Beatlemania—but ironically, it proved that the Fab Four were much, much more than a fad. The lads play themselves, more or less: running with glee and terror away from the mob and into their music.

Bull Durham *(1988)*
The best baseball movie, period. Ron Shelton's script and direction capture both the smarts and sass of the game, and Kevin Costner smolders exquisitely...until he catches fire with baseball groupie Susan Sarandon. (It's the movie where she fell for Tim Robbins, though: Go figure.)

It Happened One Night *(1934)* Claudette
Colbert and Clark Gable both resisted being cast, but director Frank Capra's revenge was sweet when his delightful early screwball romance swept the top Oscars—the only film to do so until *One Flew Over the Cuckoo's Nest* 41 years later.

The Last Picture Show *(1971)* See—movie critics *can* make great movies. Peter Bogdanovich invested the Larry McMurtry novel with a ghostly on-screen grace in this story of a dying Texas town and the teenagers (Jeff Bridges, Timothy Bottoms, Cybill Shepherd, Randy Quaid) aching to get out.

National Lampoon's Animal House *(1978)* The 1980s start right here. Messy, reactionary, stoopid, and mind-bendingly funny, John Landis' zeitgeist hit brought frat-house high jinks back into favor and made post-Woodstock pieties a thing of the past.

The Night of the Hunter *(1955)* The only film directed by actor Charles Laughton is an unsettling, gorgeously shot bedtime story about two small kids with a doll full of cash, caught between Evil (Robert Mitchum's unforgettable homicidal preacher) and Good (a radiant Lillian Gish).

Once Upon a Time in the West *(1969)* Sergio Leone made his name with a fistful of spaghetti Westerns starring Clint Eastwood, but his masterpiece is this surreal, luxuriant tall tale that pits good guy Charles Bronson against coldhearted villain Henry Fonda. Yes, *Henry Fonda*.

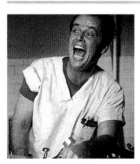

One Flew Over the Cuckoo's Nest *(1975)* Everyone's favorite movie in the mid-'70s, it marked the enshrinement of Jack Nicholson as a subversive Everyman for our age. It's also the best of a dubious movie genre—the one that says the madmen are the ones who are truly sane.

Raiders of the Lost Ark *(1981)* The heroes of Saturday-matinee serials past came roaring back to life—pumped up with special effects and gentle mockery—in Steven Spielberg's thrill ride of a movie. Looking vaguely chagrined, Harrison Ford was an ideal guide through the fun house.

Saturday Night Fever *(1977)* The movie as Moment. When John Travolta stepped into that white polyester suit and the Bee Gees kicked into the opening chords of "Stayin' Alive," an entire nation saw itself reflected in the mirror ball and headed for the dance floor.

A Star Is Born *(1954)* The story's been made and remade and *re*made, but it's the version starring Judy Garland and James Mason that best catches the blissful peaks and awful depths of life in the dream factory—not least because Garland's own demons seem to lurk so close to the surface.

A Streetcar Named Desire *(1951)* How nervous did Marlon Brando make Hollywood? Just about everyone in the brilliant film version of the play won Oscars—except for the guy who, by playing Stanley Kowalski with such searing presence, rang in a new age of screen acting.

Sullivan's Travels *(1941)* An uproarious, touching film about a comedy director who wants to get serious—made by a comedy director who wanted to get serious. Joel McCrea's the on-screen stand-in for filmmaker Preston Sturges in a crazed, soul-searching classic unlike any other movie ever made.

This Is Spïnal Tap

(1984) Turn the volume up to 11 and enjoy this fiendish mock rockumentary about the greatest heavy-metal group that never was. Rob Reiner drolly directs; Christopher Guest, Michael McKean, and Harry Shearer prance and pontificate; various drummers explode.

The Treasure of the Sierra Madre

(1948) Humphrey Bogart, Tim Holt, and Walter Huston (director John's dad, minus teeth) are the bedraggled threesome who dig for Mexican gold and watch greed and circumstance wash it all away. All together now: We don' have to show you any steenkin' badges!

The Verdict *(1982)* An

overlooked mountaintop in the careers of both director Sidney Lumet and star Paul Newman, it casts the latter as a down-and-out Boston lawyer who gets one last, troubling chance to do something right. It also has one of the movies' great open-ended closing shots.

⌃ West Side Story

(1961) A classic teen hankie wringer, the *Titanic* of its day. Natalie Wood's not Puerto Rican? Who cares? She's heartstoppingly tragic as Maria in this tenement update of "Romeo and Juliet," and the songs by Leonard Bernstein and a young Stephen Sondheim—including "Tonight," "Maria," and the rollicking "Jet Song"—are pure, beguiling ear candy.

Woman of the Year

(1942) Adam's Rib is more celebrated, but we'll take the first pairing of Spencer Tracy and Katharine Hepburn as the best. She's a political pundit, he's a sportswriter, and their relationship is a perfect, prickly fit. The scene where Kate tries to make breakfast is a stitch.

Written on the Wind

(1956) Director Douglas Sirk made big, lush, Technicolor soap operas with sharp little art movies hidden inside. This may be his peak, with Robert Stack and Dorothy Malone as tragically self-destructing siblings and Rock Hudson and Lauren Bacall as the (supposed) good guys.

159

Credits

SIDEBAR WRITERS

Carmela Ciuraru: Greatest Movies Nos. 81–85, 89; Eileen Clarke: 71–75; Matthew McCann Fenton: 1–20; Wook Kim: 59, 62–65, 96–100; Allyssa Lee: 76–80; Leslie Marable: 66–70; Joe Neumaier: 41–50, 88; Tim Purtell: 21–40, 86–87, 90; Joshua Rich: 51–58, 60–61; Erin Richter: 91–95

PHOTO CREDITS

Pages 10–11: Culver Pictures; 12: Culver Pictures; 13: Kobal Collection; 16: Photofest; 17: Kobal Collection; 18–19: (from left) Photofest; Pratarlon/Pierluigi/Reporters Associati; 22–23: MPTV (3); 24–25: (clockwise from top) Kobal Collection; Richard Miller/MPTV (2); 26–27: (clockwise from left) Marc Wanamaker/Bison Archives (2); Everett Collection; 28: Kobal Collection; 29: Photofest; 30–31: Photofest; 32–33: Kobal Collection; 34–35: (clockwise from top) Photofest; Culver Pictures (2); 36–37: (from left) MoMA/Film Stills Archive; Marc Wanamaker/Bison Archives; 38–39: (bottom, top right) ILM (2); 40–41: (from left) Kobal Collection; Archive Photos; Marc Wanamaker/ Bison Archives; 43: (from top) Everett Collection; Photofest: Everett Collection; 44: MPTV; 45: (from top) Everett Collection; Richard Miller/ MPTV; 46: Bruce McBroom/MPTV; 47: (from top) Bruce McBroom/MPTV; Kobal Collection; 48–49: (clockwise from top left) Culver Pictures; Everett Collection; Photofest; 50–51: ©Walt Disney Co./Kobal Collection (2); 52–53: (clockwise from top) Kobal Collection; MPTV; Photofest; 54–55: (clockwise from top) Foto Fantasies; MPTV; Bruce Hershenson; 56–57: MPTV (2); 58–59: (clockwise from top) MPTV; Photofest; Everett Collection; 60–61: (clockwise from top left) Everett Collection; Kobal Collection (2); MPTV; 62–63: (clockwise from left) Everett Collection; MoMA/Film Stills Archive (2); 64–65: Photofest (2); 66–67: (clockwise from left) Kobal Collection; MoMA/Film Stills Archive; Kobal Collection (2); 68: (from left) Photofest; Everett Collection; 69: Photofest; 70: Photofest; 71: Kobal Collection; 76–77: (clockwise from bottom left) Kobal Collection (2); Culver Pictures; MoMA/Film Stills Archive; 78–79: Everett Collection (3); 80–81: (from left) Photofest; MPTV; 82–83: Kobal Collection; 84–85: (clockwise from left) MPTV; Floyd McCarty/MPTV; David Sutton/MPTV; 86–87: Culver Pictures; 88–89: (from left) Photofest; Kobal Collection; 90–91: (clockwise from top left) Kobal Collection (2); Everett Collection; Kobal Collection (2); 92–93: (clockwise from left) Marc Wanamaker/Bison Archives; MoMA/Film Stills Archive; Everett Collection (2); 94–95: Bob Willoughby/ MPTV (3); 96–97: (from left) MPTV (2); MoMA/Film Stills Archive; 98: Photofest; 99: Kobal Collection; 100–101: Brian Hamill/Archive Photos (8); 102: Kobal Collection; 103: MPTV; 104–105: (from top) Kobal Collection; Everett Collection; 106: Photofest; 107: Culver Pictures; 108–109: (from left) Photofest; Kobal Collection; 110–111: (from left) Photofest; Robert Capa/Magnum Photos; 112–113: (clockwise from left) MPTV; Roman Freulich/MPTV; Kobal Collection; 114: Photofest; 115: ©Walt Disney Co.; 116: (from left) Kobal Collection; Everett Collection; 117: Everett Collection; 118–119: (from top) Everett Collection; Photofest (2); 120–121: (clockwise from left) Bill Avery/MPTV; Kobal Collection; Photofest; 122: (from left) MPTV; Culver Pictures; 123: William Read Woodfield/CPI; 124: Photofest; 125: Photofest; 126: Kobal Collection; 127: (from left) Everett Collection; Photofest; 128–129: Photofest; 130–131: (clockwise from top left) Everett Collection (2); Photofest; 132–133: (clockwise from top left) Kobal Collection (3); MPTV; 134: Steve Schapiro; 135: Everett Collection; 136–137: (from left) Everett Collection; MPTV; 138–139: Dennis Stock/Magnum Photos; Kobal Collection; 140: (from top) MPTV; Photofest; 141: (from top) Everett Collection; Kobal Collection; 142–143: (clockwise from top left) Everett Collection (2); Photofest; Everett Collection; 144–145: (clockwise from top) Photofest; Everett Collection; MPTV; 146: (from top) Photofest; MPTV; 147: (from top) Kobal Collection; Photofest; 148: Kobal Collection; 149: Photofest; 150–151: (top) Frank Connor/MPTV; 152–153: Ken Regan/Camera 5 (3); 154: Kobal Collection (2); 155: Photofest

WE DIDN'T FORGET...

Page 157: (clockwise from top left) MPTV (3); Photofest; Kobal Collection; Photofest (2); MPTV; 158: (clockwise from top left) Everett Collection (2); MPTV; Photofest; Everett Collection; Photofest; Kobal Collection; Photofest; Kobal Collection; 159: (clockwise from top) Photofest (3); Everett Collection; MPTV; Kobal Collection

FRONT/BACK OF BOOK

Page 1: Everett Collection; 2: Photofest; 6: MPTV; 160: MPTV